Love Lessons From The Cross

Reveals Seven Life Principles

Norman C. Lynch

WestBow Press books may be ordered through booksellers or by contacting:

WestBow Press
A Division of Thomas Nelson & Zondervan
1663 Liberty Drive
Bloomington, IN 47403
www.westbowpress.com
1 (866) 928-1240

ISBN: 978-1-4908-5698-8 (sc)

Library of Congress Control Number: 2014918627

Printed in the United States of America.

WestBow Press rev. date: 10/16/2014

Contents

Acknowledgements

I Thank the Lord for allowing me the privilege of sharing these insights.

These works are a new experience for me as an author and I trust your reading will excite you as much as I have enjoyed this effort.

I want to thank Dr. Brenda Lynch married for 22 years (who has also authored a great book, ("Tell –A- Vision") for all her help, from listening, to moral support.

I also appreciate the patience of my family for their encouragement over the years and those who have been waiting for this publication.

I appreciate all of the Teachers and Pastors from which I received insight and encouragement in my ministerial efforts.

In honor of my mentors who have passed; Elder William L. Jones of Springfield Ohio, Pastor Nathaniel Burleson who pastored the Mt. Rose Baptist Church, Pastor J.J. Roberson, who pastored Mt Hebron Baptist Church, Pastor emeritus Crawford Kimble, who pastored the Good Hope Baptist Church and the beloved great expositor Dr. A L. Patterson Jr., who Pastored the Mt. Corinth Baptist Church.

I also honor and thank my friends and Pastors; Robert l. Myers Sr., Dr. Kenneth Skelton of the Spirit of Life Church, and Elder Anthony Brodie, Pastor of the St. Marks Baptist Church., Pastor Alex B. Morrison Founder and Pastor of the Houston Christ way Ministries, and my current Pastor Isaac Matthews, Pastor of God's Grace Community Church of Houston.

I do trust that these words will be a blessing to many.

The Introduction

Man's idea of love has been given, received, and applauded. Man has talked about love in every language. We write about it in books, report about it in the news, sing about it in songs, and recite it in poetry. Love is the object of the deep craving of all mankind and is responded to by every creature. Receiving Love is the hope of every human heart.

Man has always needed love, from his early existence up to the "we think we are modern" days in which we live. The need for love is always painted on the countenance of many faces and is ever pounding at the hearts of a gifted and lost generation. What the world needs now is love sweet love; so the songwriter wrote and no one to my knowledge has ever disputed those words.

When we consider the impact of love in our lives, it would seem that man would consider the source from which it comes; and if you are not one to believe the word of the Lord, (The Bible) it would still seem logical to test that which claims to be. It is quite obvious by the result of man's condition, his conscience, and circumstances, that the true wisdom of love for the most part has not been regarded, received or understood.

One of the great love questions concerning life is: **Why did Christ come?** Jesus answered that question in St John 10:10 (KJV) when he said, "*I am come that **they** might have life, and that **they** might have it more abundantly.*" When Christ said he came to give life and to give it more abundantly, it was the love, which he had for and brought to mankind. When Christ said *they*, you and

I were included. We must come to him and receive his love *for us* if we are going to benefit from the fullness of his love toward us.

When we consider a list of the things Jesus said he was to do during his earthly mission, we are reminded what St. Luke 4:18 (The Message) gives us. *God's Spirit is on me; he's chosen me to preach the Message of good news to the poor, sent me to announce pardon to prisoners and recovery of sight to the blind, to set the burdened and battered free, to announce, "This is God's year to act!"* We notice that everything mentioned has the fabric of love woven within it. We first have here, **the preaching of the Gospel**, that's good news to the poor. You would certainly want to bring good news to those we love. We have also that he was sent **to heal the brokenhearted,** to preach deliverance to the captives, **recovering of sight to the blind**, to **set at liberty them that are bruised,** and to preach the acceptable year of the Lord. Each of these assignments is love driven and life giving. Life cannot produce real success without the element of love indeed. Love is the element of life that requires some form of expressive action that produces the highest benefits for the object of our love. There is a dynamic of genuine kindness woven and wrapped throughout the fabric of love. This love action is always that action which brings the best results after it has been performed or spoken. The real and rich issues of life come out of the heart, and the heart is where the love of life and the love of God rest. Solomon, (the wisest man in history) says in **Proverbs 4:23***"Keep thy heart with all diligence; for out of it are the issues of life."*

Some of the lessons we learn from the Lord's earthly assignment is love of brotherhood, the love of marriage, and many other life lessons. He also provided us with the perfect example of agape, the love of God. The scriptures are filled with examples, illustrations, and lessons on the nature of

The scriptures are not only filled with the nature of love, but it is a command from Christ Jesus that we are to love one another. We are to love with the same self-sacrificing agape love demonstrated by Christ and some of the other early church leaders. Many of the early church leaders were martyred because of their love for the Lord and the saints. St. Stephen was one martyr who had a great love for the brethren, even those who were stoning him to death. Let me share a brief summary of his life with you in **Acts 7.**Right in the heart of growth during the early church, Stephen was chosen along with six other men as administrative helpers to relieve the disciples of serving duties, (food distribution) to the widows in the church. The problems arose during that time from Greek-speaking believers toward the Hebrew-speaking believers because their widows were being discriminated against in the daily food lines. ... And so, Stephen, burning with God's grace and energy, was doing wonderful things among the people, unmistakable signs that God was among them. Stephen's actions stirred up people, the religious leaders, and religion scholars. After a long ordeal with the authorities, he was tried by those who were unable to match his wisdom and the spirit in which he spoke concerning the history and attitudes of the birth of the church; false witnesses, a mob of people, and a mock trial cause him to be stoned to death, However, before his death, the last words he shouted out to heaven was," ***Lord, lay not this sin to their charge".*** This may be a long way to the point, but this is a classic example of true love for the Lord and for the people of God. The Bible says that Stephen was full of the Holy Ghost and wisdom and an honest report among the people.

It might be wise to point out that we cannot fully love one another without first loving the God who created us. The great love commandments throughout scripture always point us to first love God, and then to love one another. Here we have God's love for us ... St John 3:16 *"For God so loved the world that he gave his only begotten son, that whosoever believeth in him should not perish, but have everlasting life."* We have a few among many scriptures commanding our love. …

St Matthew 22:37-40 (KJV) *Jesus said unto him, thou shalt love the Lord thy God with all thy heart, and with all thy soul, and with all thy mind. This is the* ***first*** *and great commandment. And the* ***second*** *is like unto it, thou shalt love thy neighbor as thyself. On these two commandments hang all the law and the prophets.*

Leviticus 19:18 (KJV) *Thou shalt not avenge, nor bear any grudge against the children of thy people, but thou shalt love thy neighbor as thyself: I am the LORD.*

IPeter1b: (KJV)…. "See that ye love one another with a pure heart fervently:" …

Ephesians 5:1, 2 (The Message) *Watch what God does, and then you do it, like children who learn proper behavior from their parents. Mostly what God does is love you.* ***Keep company with him and learn a life of love.*** *Observe how Christ loved us. His love was not cautious but extravagant. He didn't love in order to get something from us but to give everything of himself to us.* ***Love like that.*** **Colossians** 3:19 (The Message) *Husbands, go all out in love for your wives. Don't take advantage of them.* **Hebrews** 13:1 (The Message) *Stay on good terms with each other, held together* by love. … (KJV) *Let brotherly love continue.* **I John** 4:7a (KJV) *We know that we have passed from death unto life, because we love the brethren.* **Deuteronomy** 6:5. (The Message) *Love God, your God, with your whole heart: love him with all that's in you; love him with all you've got!* There are many other teaching aspects of love that I am not going to labor with here. There are seven episodes about Jesus Christ that make up his earthly incarnation, initiation, divine mission assignment and the glorious process in which they were accomplished. We know them as: **1**. The Birth at Bethlehem. **2.** The Baptism in Jordan. **3.** The Temptation in the wilderness. **4**. The Transfiguration on Mount Carmel. **5.** The Crucifixion on Golgotha's Hill 6**.** The Resurrection, and finally, 7.The Ascension. These seven episodes in the life of Jesus Christ each present a classic lesson in the library of life and love. The emphasis of this *book* is on the Love Lessons derived from the seven last words spoken by Christ from the cross at the crucifixion or the 5th episode in the initiation of our Lord's earthly ministry.

I pray that this book will be a blessing to you the reader. It is my aim to stir up your thoughts concerning the great work performed by God on our behalf. I pray that through the reading of this book, you and I both will magnify his great love toward us by sharing with the world the good news of his Magnificent Love.

Chapter One

The Prayer of Divine Love

"Then Jesus prayed, **Father, forgive them,**
for **they know not what they do.**"
Luke 23: 34

The relationship made it … uncommon
The request made for the … unrighteous
The reason made for the … unlearned

The of Prayer Divine Love

"Then Jesus prayed, Father, forgive them, for they know not what they do."
Luke 23:34 AMP

This prayer, which is also the first of the seven last statements of Jesus on the cross, gives us exposure and the expressions of the **heart of God,** and several great illustrations rich in lessons for our learning. We are given an illustration of an excellent prayer; an unselfish prayer made for those who knew neither who he was nor the God whom they thought they served. They did not know the God of Moses, and they had no clue to understanding the heart of God. The expressions made by Jesus were neither callus nor condemning toward those who were crucifying him, but rather sought to bring comfort for them. When we think of classic words and actions, this prayer would *have* to be at the top for several reasons. For one thing, it is a prayer made by the Lord Jesus Christ, *the Son of God* and the only Son of God born of a woman. The next thing is that he is on the cross performing his earthly mission in offering himself for the sin of the world. … *He is suffering.* Another classic point is the fact that those who are crucifying him are positively *included in the request* of the prayer. We see then the only begotten Son of God, hanging on a cross, suffering for the lost and at the hands of the lost, while at the same time praying on their behalf.

And so…. the lessons of love begin to spring forth from the place of redemption and the point from which all time revolve and the continuing history of Christ unwinds. We have a new dispensation with the death and resurrection of Christ. It is called the dispensation of grace. Just to make sure ... A dispensation is a period of time in which man is tested in respect of obedience to some specific revelation of the will of God. It is over the course of man's existence on earth.

This Prayer not only manifested the heart of God and his great love, but also presents several illustrations of **the power of love.** I am reminded of hearing stories of women having performed great physical acts to save their child; such as lifting an automobile alone to keep the child from being crushed. I know that you may have heard of similar stories that have been performed. These kinds of stories all have the same driving force and eternal source of power, **the power of love.** This is a divine prayer of love that also shows the power of divine love. It is love that gave the power to remain on the cross and continue to do the work of a savior. It is the same power that enables one to remain in a sacrificial condition and continue doing what is needed to maintain righteous living. It is the same power that gives strength to be faithful in our daily duties of living.

Three things we can take in consideration concerning this prayer. **1. The Wisdom and Necessity of it.** Here we see two sets of condemnation, there are the two men on their cross who know they are condemned, and the men who were participating in the crucifixion unaware of their condition. We see also two different responses and results to sin. Many of you know how the one thief *died in sin* while the other thief *died from sin*, as Christ *died for sin*. Oh! I pray that more men would see their sinful condition. The answer to that prayer was granted when men after the resurrection heard the gospel preached. Did everyone there receive it? Certainly not, and certainly not all that hear the Gospel today has received it, and the sad fact is many will hear and never receive it. Men, who are condemned and have no knowledge of their condition and what to do about it, surely need prayer. The wisdom and the necessity of the prayer were so graciously ministered for them from the heart of God, by way of his begotten son. What was needed for the helpless sinner was for someone worthy to serve the sentence of death for which man was guilty. Truly the prayer was necessary.

We consider now: **2.The Motive of it.** There is no way to get around it, and that is the fact that nothing but love in its purest form could move one to make a prayer such as this. It is as though the prayer was thought out before time, as though there was a hidden mission driving Christ to play and perform his assigned part. Moved by the force of love … Christ expresses the burden of redemption, the undying and unmovable motive that is laden deep in the depths of his bosom, moving in the very fiber of his being. It is the focuses of his passions bursting into this great love cry …father forgive them! Love *is* the greatest of all motives. Thirdly we consider: **3. The Character of it.** We cannot get away from the love factor, all three considerations. The necessity comes from the need of his helpless and ignorant created creatures that have fallen from grace without hope, Covered by God's gracious love. The motives are certainly moved by the love of God, and here we look at the Character of the prayer. Only a God could have done what was done. The character of God sets a divine standard. The character of man without God's Spirit cannot fully comprehend nor complete the standards of God. The Character of God can only bring justice and find a way to reconcile man back to himself. It is the call of his nature, His passion manifested; it is the sovereignty of his love. Love is his Character… And we see on display, the depth of love on the cross and the genius of the heart of love in the prayer.

Let us examine the prayer. The very idea of this unselfish prayer brought to mankind a whole new level of responding in the face of opposition. Notice if you will the remarkable words. ***"Father, forgive them, for they know not what they do"*** **Here** we see that the relationships are God, His Son, not the Crowd who cheered "Crucify him! Crucify him!" And so we First: point out … the **connection, and** that the ***relationship*** made it **…**

***uncommon.**" Father" Jesus* taught that we are to pray for those who persecute us, and here we see him doing just that. From an earthly view, the act of this prayer was certainly uncommon. These men who were crucifying Christ, had no relationship with God, had a hatred for Jesus, blind to the things he taught, and despised the righteousness for which his life exemplified. In this connection, the prayer made was uncommon, Jesus faced a dreadful reality, and He faced a joyful victory. It is one of his finest moments. Although it was not easy, he performed without a flaw. The fifth of a series of climactic earthly events, Note; (There are times in life when what we dread most can become some of our greatest accomplishments) His view of the sinner is rich in understanding and patience, and like a big brother or father would do, He stood in the gap and prayed on their behalf.

The example and challenge that he set before us is one of great maturity. It is the perfection of love ... The encyclopaedia ... if you will, of love. Everything we need to understand about love wrapped up in one single act on the Cross thru and by Christ Jesus. **Secondly**, we see the **content,** and the ***request*** made for the **...** ***unrighteous***. *"Forgive them"; This* may seem like an unnecessary request, in that those who needed forgiveness were *unaware of their need*. We can also say that *their heart was not **sorry** or **sensitive** toward their actions.* These two empty conditions will not cause a person to repent of their actions.

This prayer is almost a great mystery, a wonder, but when we consider who is doing the praying, it changes from a wonder to a clear and wonderful act of perfect love. It is a beloved son praying to an all-powerful, loving Father, who is God. Men who crucified Jesus are the same men today, who refuse to acknowledge and/or believe who Jesus is and who despise what he brings to life. Herein lays the great sin and the one reason the prayer was needed. The sin is that of unbelief, but the sin has a blinding effect so much so that the unbeliever cannot see or understand his condition. Just to make sure *the word blind or blindness is used both physically and metaphorically, mostly in the New Testament. It comes from the Greek word porosis. This is a medical term that means a covering with a callus, a hardening. It is a spiritual and mental blockage. Metaphorically of a dulled spiritual perception,* Mark 3:5 (RV) *"at the hardening of their hearts;"*

Jesus Christ prayed and died for those who were crucifying him, and also for those today that are in the same sinful condition without knowledge. It is a classic presentation of the Righteous dying for the unrighteous. It was the innocent suffering for the guilty. His request was that they might be pardon because of Him. He received penalty (payment) for their actions; therefore, allowing justice to fall on him instead of on the guilty.

Thirdly, we consider … **The contention, and** the ***reason*** made for the ***… unlearned.*** *"for they know not what they do"* How can they know accept they be taught. At the point of the cross, men was staring the beauty of the Gospel in the face, but did not know, because of their blindness, which was caused by their unbelief.

Ephesians 4: 18 ***"Having the understanding darkened, being alienated from the life of God through the ignorance that is in them, because of the blindness of their heart:"***

This is truly the heart of a divine Savior, who recognizes the desperate need of his creation. Jesus **pleads for the sinner**; he **dies for the sinner** and becomes the **sin of the sinner**. It is his great love that contends … they cannot make this plea, they do not even understand, for they are lost in the darkness of their unbelief. Let me point out that this unlearned status is somewhat different from a mere lack of information, but a deliberate rejection of the presented truth. It is the same attitude and action taken by Adam. He knew the truth and the consequences of disobeying God, but chose to follow the persuasion of Satan by way of Eve. His knowledge and his actions were deliberate sin that God did judge and will continue to judge.

We cannot expect the ignorant to know what has not been revealed any more than we can expect a child to be accountable for the things that has not been taught them. The parent stands responsible for the actions of an infant as well as for a child that may still be at the age of innocence. That can also hold true in regard to a teacher and the student who enters the class for study on the first day. Life is set up on that principle.... And so we see that the one is truly a state of innocence and ignorance...while the former is that of rebellion, because they refuse to accept what has been presented, the act of deliberate rebellion makes one guilty of sin. James writes, "*Therefore to him that knoweth to do good, and doeth it not, to him it is sin.*" James 4:17 (KJV)

I ought to qualify what may possibly be an avenue of misunderstanding here. Sin and ignorance both carries consequence. When you have erred from the truth of life because of ignorance, the end is the same as if you knew. There may be a slight difference in the degree based on your exposure to the truth. Dr. Luke helps us here in 12:47,48a (The Message) The *servant who knows what his master wants and ignores it, or insolently does whatever he pleases, will be thoroughly thrashed. But if he does a poor job through ignorance, he'll get off with a slap on the hand. Great gifts mean great responsibilities; greater gifts, greater responsibilities!*

I might also add that in this life, we run the danger of losing our life when we think and try to live an unrighteous life hoping that the Lord will rescue us when death stares us in the face. The world of drugs, the world of prostitution, homosexuality and lesbianism are some of the great strong holds that satan has on many. These worlds and others are tremendous cesspools that have sucked in and influenced many in every generation. Too many God given talents are lost to this kind of cesspool damnation. The effects of these outward influences that are experienced by the human body have caused the inward man to become torn and bitter, apathetic and cold hearted. It has helped develop a selfish greed and an ungodly conscious capable of anything from habitual lying to conspiratorial murder on a mass basis.

The possibilities of real success in life are found in the hearing, believing and receiving the good news of Jesus Christ. It is Christ (*the anointed One*) dying on the cross that gives us the clearing and cleansing opportunity to face God and to face life in spite of the world's we may have been through. Unrepented and unforgiven sin will face the death of the justice of God. The only way for sin to be removed is for an acceptable sacrifice be made to God for the remission (*Clearance*) of our sins. That offering is what Christ has done for us by giving his life for our sins. Romans 6:23 (KJV) ***"For the wages of sin is death; but the gift of God is eternal life through Jesus Christ our Lord."***

We see now the far-reaching effects of the Savior's prayer. If he had not died for the sinner, the sinner would die because of his ignorance, and of his sin. We are reminded of the words of Jesus in St. John 8:32 *"And you shall know the truth, and the truth shall make you free."* You shall be made free from sin and the end of sin, which is death.

The cross and the resurrection are the turning points from the curse of spiritual blindness; it is the revealed power over unbelief … the manifested power of the love of God … the expressed actions of God's sovereignty. It was all done on our behalf.

There is one thing for sure and that is we all stand in the need of a Savior. There is actually no excuse for man to be lost, especially after hearing and understanding the Gospel. We can choose to believe or reject the good news of salvation. We read in Romans 3:23 (KJV) *"For all have sinned, and come short of the glory of God:"* ***This*** great love that the Lord has demonstrated toward us, gives us an opportunity to escape the eternal wrath of God. Mmm…if this was not a book, I would shout hallelujah.

St. John 3:16 "*For God so loved the world, that he gave his only begotten Son, that whosoever believeth in him should not perish but have everlasting life.*"

We now briefly consider the overall principles presented for practice. The fundamental acts of the God of grace are full of lessons to be observed and absorbed. There are several presentations of Christ throughout the scriptures, here we point to Him as The Christ of the Cross, The pre-eminent Saviour, The final hope of re- conciliation between God and man.

Chapter Two

The Promotion of Delegated Love

"When Jesus therefore saw his mother, and the disciple, standing by, whom he loved, he saith unto his mother, Woman, behold thy son! Then saith he to the disciple, Behold thy mother! And from that hour that disciple took her unto his own home."
John 19: 26, 27

A Divine Assignment …for all life
A Dedicated Analysis … for actual living
A Deeper Association … in achieving love

The Promotion of Delegated Love

"When Jesus therefore saw his mother, and the disciple, standing by, whom he loved, he saith unto his mother, Woman, behold thy son! Then saith he to the disciple, Behold thy mother! And from that hour that disciple took her unto his own home."
St John 19: 26, 27

There is a divine assignment attached to every soul, and life is full of choices in connection with the assignment. Here we see the concern and the care Jesus expressed for his mother. We see also the assignment given both to her and to John to behold one another in a different or perhaps on an elevated level.

There is no doubt that John and the other disciples had great respect for Mary the mother of their leader, however; this command was a Promotion and a Delegated Love. This is an active gesture of love that would last a lifetime. A hands on demonstration of I care for those of whom you care, and I care enough to fill in with the comforts, the care and the protections of everyday life. This subtle yet brilliantly displayed lesson from the Master rings loudly from Golgotha's hill of pain and Joy. This specialized assignment given to his mother Mary and his friend and disciple John was also an eternal command to every **Woman of a Godly Conscious** and to every **Man Reborn of Wisdom;** it is to you that this promotion is delegated. …Behold ***thy Son… Behold thy Mother!*** There are many mothers in the world today who was unable to bare children from their own bodies, but who still care for children because of the love they have for children in their heart. It is the natural element of motherhood that constrains them to want to care for children. There are also women who have somehow lost the natural affection and passion to turn their love toward children, who would rather pursue other avenues of life. These assignments given to us are given while we are still in our mother's womb, way before we are conscious of the plan for our life. The purpose for our birth is there all the time, lying dormant, waiting to be stirred and developed unto the fullness of our assignment. It is a tragedy to go through life and never become aware of the fundamental purpose for which we are allowed to enter the world. This command goes out into a world that is challenged by satan to be conformed to a society that he dictates.

There is a great possibility that John did a great job in fulfilling his personal assignment in connection to Mary; However, When Jesus gave this command he knew that everyone, for whatever reason, would not successfully complete their assignment. The good news is we can be assured that God knows our heart and the efforts we put forth in trying. God knows the road we have had to travel; He knows how we were molded and how rough and how detrimental the unrighteous molding may have been. Many men, women, and children have been treated so unloving in their childhood and left with no resistance against the traps and strongholds of satan as they tried to move through a cold perverted, and uncaring society.

And so Christ gave this command that it might help us exercise love for one another in a special way and perhaps as Christians should. This command takes away the selfish thinking that I can only help those to whom I am connected biologically. It pushes away the selfish idea that I should only help those that may be able to return the favor or perhaps there may be some financial benefit if I do.

Many drug users were taken through such emotional drama in their early life that they have never as of now found their niche in life; in fact they were never able to focus on anything except to try an escape the pain. Jesus suffered in every area that we have been, all of us; Therefore, He understands our situations and circumstances. He also knows that there are those who wanted to complete their assignment for those who have discovered it, and he knows there are those who have only been trying to escape the pain. He knows they carry pain in their heart because they have not been as spiritually productive as they would like to have been. It is the heart that God judges when it comes to relationships, starting with our relationship with him. In a very significant way our love and life is measured by how we strive to keep the commandment of treating others the way we would like to be treated. Jesus said, "Love the Lord your God with all your passion and prayer and intelligence.' This is the most important, the first on any list. But there is a second to set alongside it: 'Love others as well as you love yourself.' These two commands are pegs; everything in God's Law and the Prophets hangs from them." Our ability to complete our divine assignments is inextricably tied into our efforts to maintain relationships, and to obey the commandments of our Lord. I must point out that when we are born, we have the God given ability to perform the God given assignment for our life. It is the influence of satan, the temptations and tribulations of this world that causes defeat, delay and deterrence.

Only by receiving the love of God in our hearts will we have the strength to perform as God has designed and as we may passion to do.

There is another issue that I want to address here. With this command we here the underlying argument that he may not have come from your womb; maybe not, but he is still your son, he may be from another culture, but yet, he is your son. His nationality may be unfamiliar with yours, His schooling and upbringing may have been from another country and/or mindset, (He may be very difficult to deal with, and may not be reaching for much in life), but he too was made in the image and likeness of God. He was brought forth to bring glory to God and should be treated as a … son! It may have to be at a distance, but when the occasion passes our way, the meeting, the encounter should be that of kindness mixed with the readiness to show charity and share wisdom.

The argument is no less for men if not greater. You, the Man Reborn of God, or you who want to be wise, is the intended leaders and protectors of the women that God made for our glory. I Corinthians 11:7 (KJV) …" ***but the woman is the glory of the man***" The woman was made to be loved and cared for. They are to be respected and uplifted for their efforts and for the joy that they were designed to bring. She may not have lived in the house with you, but she is to be treated like a mother. She to may not be understood by culture, but it is your command to treat her with a Godly respect. You may not agree on many things, but God has made her to be your helper in life … She is your mother. She has labored to raise up your brother … She is your mother. She may be struggling in life and with life, yes I know, but if she has borne and labored to raise a child, it is your brother or your sister, treat her as a mother. The current status in her life is not the issue to be highlighted, though it may become a concern; we are not always aware of the road one has traveled to get to where they are.

Widows, Orphans, and the poor are souls that life's struggles have created, through which God has made available for many to serve. When we talk about widows, orphans and the poor, they hold a very special place in the heart of God. They are mentioned throughout the scriptures to be the target of our charity. James 1:27 (KJV) ***"Pure religion and undefiled before God and the Father is this, to visit the fatherless and widows in their affliction, and to keep himself unspotted from the world."*** They are the least of these that Jesus referred and that we can touch Him by touching them. Let us turn now to the outlined principles to help in gleaning these assignments. There are three great noticeable principles in our assigned focus. **First** we see that this was **A Divine Assignment … for all life.** It was a divine command from a dying Savior. Life is to be lived unselfishly. It is also crucial that we live in and thru relationships. We can safely say that Jesus assigns the care of women to men of God with the same respect and love you would have for your own. The assignments bestowed on our life have several basic areas of focus. Jesus changes the relationship between his mother and John by presenting John as Her son. He then confirms the relationship by presenting his mother as John's. We are not surprised at this or the response from John. The scripture tells us that John took Mary that very day into his own home. This was a ***divine assignment*** *from* the Lord. John was the friend of Jesus, but John was not asked to care for the mother of the Savior, He was given an assignment.

We also notice that this was a **Dedicated Analysis ... for actual living.** This was an assignment for John and for John alone. Jesus obviously trusted John as a good provider and protector. This is a ***dedicated*** assignment because that is what it will take to complete it, dedication. Jesus was not the only son of Mary's, he was only the first-born, and it would seem that there might have been other options for the assignment. The option of choosing one of the other sons and those considerations may have been seriously taking into mind, but after all things had been weighed, the decision for this life lasting responsibility came to John, in the final analysis, it was John who got the assignment. Assignments come and go. Assignments are a part of our ***actual living.***

Our life is measured by the way we actually live and relate to others. ***I John 3; 14 We know that we have passed from death unto life, because we love the brethren. He that loveth not his brother abideth in death.*** The assignments we encounter in life may be challenging, but no assignment is greater than our capacity to complete it. The Lord knows what is needed for our growth and many assignments are specifically designed for that purpose. The ways we involve ourselves in relationships are most important. Our spiritual maturity is measured somewhat in how we handle relationships. We can be skilled and brilliant in the affairs of this world, but if we know not how to relate to or have sensitivity toward others, the truth about our maturity has yet to be realized. We may think we are mature because of some outward act of gift giving or our display of a God given talent, but the fundamental kindness and caring that's wrapped up in basic relational skills may be suffering much.

There is now a higher level of respect John has for Mary. He not only sees her as a Godly woman, but now as his own mother. John's responsibility has now changed from the question "How is your mother doing? To, "Thank you Lord for giving me what we need to continue living a blessed life." The responsibility has move to another level.

We see thirdly, that it is a ***Deeper Association … in achieving love.*** It is a wonderful thing to see how the love of God operates at its highest level. Standing in the shoes of another and taking on their responsibilities changes the association. It would seem that blood should be thicker than friendship, however; the love of God can cause one to function on the highest degree of grace, and cause those who may be unrelated to serve one another on that divine level.

The association between John and Mary has painted the true picture of a portion of the passion of the heart of God. The Lord has a special concern for the feeble, the orphans and widows. In fact, the Bible gives us a lot of examples of how to care for them. We go again to the book of James (The Message) 1:27 ***"Pure religion and undefiled before God and the Father is this, to visit the fatherless and widows in their affliction, and to keep himself unspotted from the world."*** Mary was already a widow, Joseph her husband has died, and now her first-born son is hanging on the cross dying for the sins of the world. Certainly Jesus was a special child to Mary. He was a special child given to the world and so his death must have been very heavy to witness and endure. In this episode of sorrow, Mary and John have just gone through a common bonding, and I venture to say had some bearing on this divine assignment. When we consider the uniqueness of his death, there is a twofold emotion that rises in the spirit and soul of the believer. There are also great emotions displayed by the LORD. Isaiah 53:10 (KJV) ***"Yet it pleased the LORD to bruise him; he hath put him to grief: when thou shalt make his soul an offering for sin, he shall see his seed, he shall prolong his days, and the pleasure of the LORD shall prosper in his hand".*** Also in The Message Isaiah 53:10 ***"Still, it's what God had in mind all along, to crush him with pain. The plan was that he gave himself as an offering for sin so that he'd see life come from it- life, life, and more life. And God's plan will deeply prosper through him.*** It is a sorrowful emotion because of the pain and suffering that Jesus had to endure. Mary and John both had heavy hearts standing at the cross. It was an experience no one would want to witness of a friend, especially one who meant so much. There was also great joy at the cross. The love of God for humanity outweighed the process of pain needed to rescue a dying world without hope. The assignment, which was taken by Christ Jesus, was also analyzed for the good of the sinner. There was no other man born of a woman that could have been made a sacrifice for sin. Sinful man needed a sinless lamb, and Christ came to be that innocent lamb for us.

And so we see that the divine assignments given to us are given for all life. It is the makeup of our being. The way God has designed and equipped us to function in life. All creatures have their assignments to be enjoyed. They are to be productive with what God has given. The assignments are to all life, the beast of the field, the birds of the air, the world of water and all its inhabitants, and certainly to us who are made in the image and likeness of God our Creator.

The assignments are for actual everyday living. The road we travel is carved out for the purpose of accomplishing our divine assignments. The beauty of all things working in harmony with the universe and in harmony with all of God's creation has to be a magnificent idea to consider and the ultimate and ideal picture of mankind in bringing glory to God. The genius of God's creation designed everything capable of performing at a high standard that would bring him glory and bring us great joy.

When we talk about assignments, and when we talk about making provisions for saving the world, this assignment and accomplishment on the cross is it!

The Lord knew we needed to learn how to love. He has given us a great example and this assignment given to John and Mary gives us some detail examples in the area of relationships of what we should be willing to do.

Chapter Three

The Promised Destiny of Love

And Jesus said unto him, Verily I say unto thee, today shalt thou be with me in paradise.
St Luke 23; 43

He recognized his grievous condition … as a sinner
His request was granted for conversion … salvation
He received grace and comfort … from the savior

The Promised Destiny of Love

And Jesus said unto him, Verily I say unto thee,
Today shalt thou be with me in paradise.
St Luke 23; 43

We have here the words of comfort spoken from The Incarnate Son of God, The Christ, while in the process of dying. This is the response to a request made by one of the prisoners hanging on the cross next to Jesus. Dr. Luke gives us the reasons for which Jesus was born, and here until the very end of his life, He performs. ***St. Luke 4: 18*** *The spirit of the Lord is upon is me, because he hath anointed me* ***to preach the gospel to the poor;*** *he hath sent me* ***to heal the brokenhearted,*** *to* ***preach deliverance to the captives,*** *and* ***recovering of sight*** *to the blind,* ***to set at liberty*** *them that are bruised, To preach the* ***acceptable year*** *of the Lord.*

It was a spoken promise based on the grace side of God's great love. We see here ourselves before our encounter with Christ. It is perhaps before we heard the power of the gospel. While we were guilty of everything we were bold enough to do. While we were hateful, mean, liars, alcoholics, drugs users, women and men chasers, and you name it;

The Cross of Christ, the Love of God, stood and yet stands waiting on the unrepented to come. It was when we were yet in our sins, that Christ died for us as is with these thieves. God blessed the one with the wisdom to call on the saviour with the faith (*action to call on him*) to believe that somehow his request would get a response. The thief was included in this great love gift before he called out to be remembered.

These two guilty men, one on the right and the other on the left were both sentence to die alone with Jesus. The first thief was one that did not believe that Jesus was the Christ. He spoke to Jesus as to say *if you are* who you say you are, then prove it by saving yourself and us. There was unbelief in the heart of this sinner. He only wanted to come down from the cross, perhaps so he could continue his previous life style.

It is a dangerous thing to be insubordinate to authority; not to mention speaking to the Lord in a disrespectful manner. The tone and timbre in which this unbelieving thief spoke to Jesus was one of scoffing and scorn. The word is railing, which carries the idea of attack without patience; to demand an action to push for proof without kindness or any effort to understand.

The real issue of our concern here is not the first thief, but the dialogue between the second thief and Christ. The passionate word of promise from the dying Savior brings added Light and Life to the act of Love, even until death. This word from the master really gives us a beautiful window view at the love of God. It is a change in the scenery light. It is the same love, but painted with a different shade of emotional charity. The word is re-conciliation. It is part of the fundamental reason God set up the plan of salvation. (Just a note here) When Adam broke the natural and spiritual relationship with God by willfully disobeying, a separation took place, a brake in the closeness between God and man. Adam's sin created hostility between God and man, but the cross is the source of peace. The sin was punishable by death, and Jesus died for us so that we might live and have peace with God. The Lord God began the plan of salvation so that man could have the opportunity to be reconciled back to the relationship that was broken by Adam. The Lord is very passionate about having the right relationship with us. IICorinthians 5:20, 21 (KJV) *Now then we are ambassadors for Christ, as though God did beseech **you** by us: we pray **you** in Christ's stead, be ye reconciled o God. For he hath made him **to be** sin for us, who knew no sin; that we might be made the righteousness of God in him. Also* Ephesians 2:16-18 (The Message) *Christ brought us together through his death on the cross. The Cross got us to embrace, and that was the end of the hostility. Christ came and preached* *peace to you outsiders and peace to us insiders. He treated us as equals, and so made us equals. Through him we both share the same Spirit and have equal access to the Father.* Christ's death on the cross has made it possible for man to return to God and still live. Without the cross we must remember Romans 6:23 (The Message) *Work hard for sin your whole life and your pension is death, but God's gift is life, eternal life, delivered by Jesus our Master.*

Jesus Response to the one thief was words of comfort and promise. "Today shalt thou be with me in paradise." Let us examine the mental process of the thief. We are told by two of the other gospel writers that both thieves reviled Jesus at the beginning of their crucifixion, Matthew 27:44 Mark 15:32. There was obviously a change of heart with one of the thieves and he turns on the other with rebuke and calls on Jesus for redemption. Luke 23: 42 "And he said unto Jesus, Lord, remember me when thou comest into thy kingdom".

This request and response from this dying criminal reveals several rich principles and gives more insight to the work of Christ. We point **first** to the fact that He **Recognized his Grievous *Condition* ... as a Sinner.** Many are in a pitiful spiritual state but sadly are unaware of their condition. This first point of discussion gives the reason for his call. The scriptures can help us find ourselves. They are a world of answers, a world of comforts and many other wonderful cures; but those who would profit most seldom visit the world of the scriptures. This thief, though he may not have known the scripture, was saved by a scripture principle. We have here a sincere call of a repented heart. Once the thief understood whom Jesus was, the tone of his tongue changed to the sounds of a contrite heart which Jesus was quiet familiar. The love of God reached out to this call, put death on hold and continued to work on the plan for which he came. This thief became aware of his condition and his ultimate destination far beyond the cross. He realized his grievous condition and it was too hard for him to deal with. He probably could not explain it to well at this junction, but he believed that Jesus was who he claimed to be and called on him as his Lord.

When we are in our right mind, our decisions concerning our salvation should not be based on the opinions of others. The foolish railings that was shouted at Jesus from the crowd and the other thief was an influence for a while to this thief, but after he watched the actions or response from Jesus and felt the attitude of his presence, he came to himself and made a lifesaving decision.

Here is a lesson worth noting, and there are several ways to say it. Evil communication corrupts. Satan's main purpose is to mislead and create doubt in that which will do you the most good. Anyone aggressively opposed to the scriptures is against him and the Bible calls them an antichrist.

We now look, **secondly** at the response from the Lord Jesus. He is the savior of the world to those who call on him, and here in the midst of his giving himself for the sins of world the savior listen to the call of the thief/criminal hanging to die for his sins. Christ, the Anointed One heard him and … **His Request was Granted for Conversion … Salvation.** It is true, if we call, He will answer. He is not short of his promise. He answered then and he will answer even today, when the call from a sincere heart is heard, salvation is granted. I must point out that the thief done nothing to be worthy of salvation. All he did was to believe and call on the name of the Lord. It is a remarkable thought that salvation is just a call away. Ephesians 2:8, 9 (KJV) *For by grace are we saved through faith; and that not of yourselves: it is the gift of God: Not of works, lest any man should boast."* salvation is just a sincere call away. I would think that this thief was as sincere as it comes, after all he is dying and no one had ever been taken down from crucifixion because they were given mercy after being convicted. Apostle Paul Quoted from Joel 2:32 when writing to the churches in Rome. Romans10: 13 (KJV) *"For whosoever* *shall call upon the name of the Lord shall be saved."* What we witness here in the scriptures continues the display of the heart of God thru Jesus Christ. We see his great love magnified by an act of grace, an act of continuing his earthly mission, an act of Divine Goodness, and the act of a sovereign God right down to the very end. Hebrews 13:8 (KJV) let us know that there is no change in Christ Jesus. "*Jesus Christ the same yesterday, and today, and forever.*" And so the call to Jesus from the dying thief resulted in the fact that Salvation is a call away. Lest I bore you, **Thirdly,** we look now at the result of his call. We see that **He Received Grace and Comfort … from the Savior.** As wonderful as this act may seem to have been at this junction for the thief, it is no more than what the Lord is doing today for everyone and anyone that will call on him from a sincere heart. We may not be hanging from a literal tree, but many are hanging spiritually from the dreads sinful conditions. I can assure you that it does not matter where you are or what you have done in days gone by, you are not out of the reach of God' love. ***He received grace.*** Grace is something we receive that we really don't deserve. It comes out of the love of God. Grace is part of God's personality. It is the foundation upon which we have been given by God to build our spiritual structures of life. He not only received grace but he now has great **comfort** in knowing his destiny will be a joyful place. **How good is God!**

This word paradise just *sounds* like a great place to look forward to." The word paradise is an oriental word, first used by the historian Xenophon, denoting the parks of Persian kings and nobles. Here the promise of the Lord to the repentant robber was fulfilled the same day; Christ, at his death, having committed His spirit to the Father, went in spirit immediately into Heaven itself, the dwelling place of God (the Lord's mention of the place as Paradise must have been a great comfort to the malefactor; to the oriental mind it expressed the sum total of blessedness).

I must say it again; it is by grace that we are saved through faith and that not of our own. And so this thief has been converted from a sinner to a child of God's simply by the faith he showed and spoke to Christ while dying on a cross.

In connection to response, it must have been so that all through the process of Christ's earthly ministry he constantly had the plan of salvation and the purpose for which he came at the forefront of his mind. Although the one purpose of his coming can be summed up in that he came to minister to the whole man. He ministered to man's spirit, soul and body.

Just to recap this response by Jesus from the request of the thief. We see that **First** the thief recognized his grievous condition as a sinner. The noticeable principle here: We must also become aware of our spiritual position and condition. **Secondly**, after he saw his condition and understood his destination, he made a request to be saved. The request made by the thief was based on his faith that Jesus was the Christ. The lord granted his request based on the fulfilling of the promise of salvation. Here again we to must believe as the thief, that Jesus is the Christ, The Son of God, raised to bring life to a dying world. And **finally**, not only was he heard, but also he received more than he determined or deserved, he received the Grace of God and the comfort of knowing that his eternal destination had just been changed. We must consider that all he had done was wiped away, covered by the blood of Christ, our sacrificial lamb. What he received was so much more than he could have ever worked for. The (Message) says "… *All we do is trust him enough to let him do it. It's God's gift from start to finish! We don't play the major role. If we did, we'd probably go around bragging that we'd done the whole thing! No, we neither make nor save ourselves. God does both the making and saving. He creates each of us by Christ Jesus to join him in the work he does, the good work he has gotten ready for us to do, work we had better be doing."* It is God's redeeming plan and process to reconcile man with and to him.

Chapter Four

The Perplexed Difficulties of Love

Eli, Eli, lama sabacthani? … My God, My God, why hast thou forsaken me?
Matthew 27: 46

The fullness of Despair … A Pilgrimage to Grace
The fact of Desertion … Plan on this Grief
The feeling of Depression … Process of Growth

The Perplexed Difficulties of Love

Eli, Eli, lama sabacthani? … My God, My God, why hast thou forsaken me?
Matthew 27:46

Love is the strongest element of life. It brings to us the greatest joys in life but it can also bring the greatest sorrows. We find here a personal and painful cry from the heart of God (Jesus Christ) to God. It may be difficult comprehend, but in addition to the pain, this experience brought *pleasure* to God as well. The beautiful Bible reference says so much in this connection: Isaiah 53: "…. The cry from Jesus carries with it the plea from and of the world for the **Grace** of life. His cry was also made while **Mercy** vicariously carries the great weight of the sins of the world. That includes yours and mind. He cries while **Justice** applies the gavel of Devine righteousness in the courtroom of eternity. This great suffering moment brings together the fullness of God's personality all wrapped in this expression of true Love on the highest level possible, Agape. And so we see these two spiritual sisters at work, doing what they do, **Grace** giving life to the undeserved, **Mercy** holding back that which the guilty should be getting, but not at the expense of their big brother, **Justice**. These are the fundamental ingredients of love, even agape love.

Love is used to bring the best out of every soul. When there is love in the heart, there is hope. When there is an element of love connected with any task, the best efforts will usually show up. When there is love for a person, no challenge or task seems to be too difficult to face. There are times when a project or job may be dreaded or despised, but because of the benefits it brings for the one we love, we somehow find the strength to continue as long as necessary. If there is an end reward, or a prize to gain; although the classes may be difficult to pass or a hard fought game to win, you can be sure that love is the source of continued strength for the challenge. When the cause is in the heart, and the will has been settled, only weakness, injury or death will alter the outcome.

There are times and may I add many times in life when the love journey of life brings what seems to be an unbearable weight of pain. Jesus reminds us that our love for him is evidenced in our willingness and ability to obey his commandments. **St. John** 14: 15(KJV) *"If ye love me, keep my commandments"*. (The Message) *"If you love me, show it by doing what I've told you"*. We have here a deep inner passion of pain. The pain of being deserted can bring a great sense of low self-esteem. Low self-esteem can be caused in many ways and desertion is an element of life that can certainly bring that challenge.

There is a universal statement that no man is an island, and that is a true statement, however; life brings opportunities for growth through walking some roads alone. There are many times and things life brings that only you can do and only you must face. The good news is that after you have gone through them, you have also had an opportunity to learn and grow in the process.

When you were a child, only you could grow through the wisdom-tooth process, or face the needles needed to immune you from many childhood illnesses. Jesus gives us a great example in facing the process and going through the things that are difficult to face. He focused on the mission and the results that follow. Hebrews 12:2-3 (KJV) says, *"Looking unto Jesus, the author and finisher of our faith; who for the joy that was set before him endured the cross, despising the shame, and is set down at the right hand of the throne of God. For consider him that endured such contradiction of sinners against himself, lest ye be wearied and faint in your minds."* The Message Bible renders the same scripture as, *"Keep your eyes on Jesus, who both began and finished this race we're in. Study how he did it. Because he never lost sight of where he was headed – that exhilarating finish in and with God – he could put up with anything along the way: Cross, shame, whatever. And now he's there, in the place of honor, right alongside God. When you find yourselves flagging in your faith, go over that story again, item by item, that long litany of hostility he plowed through. That will shoot adrenaline into your souls!"*

There are turning points in life that bring us to a solemn reality that we have done all that we can do. Or that we have hit the brick wall for the last time, we have bottomed out – stressed out, if you will. Our reason for living has been challenged to its very end. The reasons may differ, the magnitude and method of the crossroads may have come from any of life's diverse avenues, but the cry from each comes from the corner called the ***Fullness of Despair***.

It does not come with favor to economics nor is it exclusive to those in prestigious positions. But, for many, the dead end street becomes the place from which we reach the wake-up point in our lives, whereas we may be deep in the darkness, yet we see the light of grace waiting to be embraced and to embrace us with the comforting companionship of God's Love.

We have come to the ***Fullness of Despair*** … which I submit to you is a ***Pilgrimage to Grace***… This is a principle of life. Before we are elevated to becoming co-workers with God, we must first come to a point of surrender. When Jesus said, "Blessed are the poor in Spirit," he refers to those who have surrendered themselves to God, they have been humbled by the grace of God, and they depend on God to save them. There are several avenues that bring us to this point of despair.

It is interesting when we consider the difference in how and when this point in life is met. Some may travel long and hard, rough and despairing, before they let go of those things in life that keep God's saving Grace at a distance. There are others who surrender early in life, and in so doing, bypass much unnecessary heartache. They not only keep much unnecessary heartache from themselves, but for those with whom they are associated.

The fullness of despair, though it may be heavy in our spirit, does not have to be a dead end or brick wall experience. But it is through and to the end of self-efforts that the successful pilgrimage to grace is made. Jesus has given us a great example of coming to the loneliness of the 'all I can do' struggles of life. No nobler mission has ever been assigned. We must understand that the despair that met Christ at the cross, which Jesus was born to bear, was delivered by way of the sins of the world? All along Christ's earthly incarnation and the magnificent exhibition of facing earthly challenges while performing comforting and life-giving acts is his ***Pilgrimage to Grace*** that has been extended to all mankind. 2Peter 3:9 (The Message)*He is restraining himself on account of you, holding back the End because he doesn't want anyone lost. He's giving everyone space and time to change.*

The pilgrimage to grace is the journey thru life that eventually brings us face to face with the Lord and continues after. There will always be hills to climb and challenges to overcome; it is part of life's journey. We must first overcome satan's attempts to keep us from yielding to the Lord, and after we do, we must overcome satan's attempts to keep us unproductive.

It is important for us to know that when we stumble or do wrong, we ask God to forgive us, and we must *mean that from the heart.* It is the purity of the heart that the Lord weighs. *Galatians 6:7 (KJV) "Be not deceived; God is not mocked: for whatsoever a man soweth, that shall he also reap."* The Message Bible is like this:" *Don't be misled: No one makes a fool of God. What a person plants, he will harvest."*

There is another point of consciousness and that is **The Fact of Desertion ... Plan on this Grief.** The fact of desertion is an all-day everyday affair throughout the world. Desertion does not necessarily mean you are alone or that a person has purposely left someone not to return. It does mean you are alone; however, you may be in the middle of a crowd or maybe on stage as the main attraction, you may be staying or living with someone at the same address, while all along, you are *alone*. Desertion has set in because of the lack of the basic necessities of life.

There is the fact of spiritual desertion, which exists whenever, and wherever certain social elements are missing. These life-supporting elements are essential for companionship. When there is **no** one to **dialogue** with, to hear your personal passions, when what you have to share with a certain group or individual is scarcely or never made possible, **no** personal **share time**, these are forms of desertion.

Many families are deserted by well meaning family members who are either always of too often busy working on stuff. This stuff you can be assured of is that cannot give back in the form of feelings and appreciation. I'm sure you know, the work on the job, the maintenance of the house, certainly the washing and care of the car, my hair, my nails, These and many more things to do like them help carve the desertion of many lonely hearts who have more time and things to talk about than there are those to arrange time to hear. And so I wonder *Mr. and Mrs. GotLotsofImportantThingsToDo*; you may argue this, but are you saying "these people are not that important that I would carve out time in my busy schedule to spend time with them, or I'm really not that interested in what they want to talk about, even if it is a passionate subject to *them*. I understand that my time may cause their life to become more meaningful in they're growing up, or my positive input may boost the creativity of some thinking mind, but I'm too busy doing *things*. For me to take my God given time and invest it in *people* goes against what I want to do, family or no family, I have things to accomplish.

It is here that we can see part of the heavy emotional load that Christ Jesus carried, from the time he entered the planet until this climaxing episode on the cross, for he had become accustomed to being deserted. I know he had crowds at times around him, but in the midst of the crowd many times there was a man who was alone. He was deserted by not being heard, deserted by unbelief, deserted by rejection, deserted by not being understood, and by any other way we might experience. One of the tests of discipleship was a point in case when Jesus was deserted or rejected three times. His answer to those who applied to follow him: Mathew 8:20 (KJV) "…***The foxes have holes, and the birds of the air have nests; but the Son of man hath not where to lay his head."*** The Message***, Jesus was curt: "Are you ready to rough it? We're not staying in the best inns, you know.***"

There is the abandonment of desertion, but there are so many other ways as well. In fact when desertion is experienced while staying at the same address, it's hard to imagine the daily hope and disappointments a person must go through and particularly a child. An adult can make the necessary adjustments by turning to someone else or some organization or getting involved with some group or even with a church family; however, the desertion of children lays the foundation for so much more in regards to future vulnerability. (So much would I love to discuss that subject here, but very soon I will write concerning our children if the Lord says the same.)

Finally, Let us consider: **The Feeling of Depression … Process of Growth.** There were times in the life of Jesus when he had the feeling of depression. Jesus was born of a woman, and according to Job (KJV) 14:1 *"Man that is born of a woman is of few days, and full of trouble."* The (Message) "*We're all adrift in the same boat: too few days, too many troubles."* This certainly holds true for our Savior. Depression may have been one of the feelings Jesus was familiar with, but it did not dominate his life nor did it keep him from fulfilling his divine assignment while here on earth. His life was the life of the Master Teacher, and he has vividly taught us the walk of love. Here we see that love finishes in spite of the difficulties from outside forces or inner challenges. He reminds us that the power we possess within is greater than life's struggles, inside or out. Christ has overcome the world; therefore, he encourages us to trust God and be faithful in well doing.

There are trials and troubles in life that we must go through in order to grow; this feeling of depression is one, and having the ability to experience the feeling of depression without falling out of life brings growth to the soul and helps clear seating for wisdom. And so this feeling of depression I submit is a process of growth. It is an opportunity for spiritual growth, which is needed and can only come through the classroom of life. Wisdom comes from God. There are levels or degrees of wisdom given when the student is prepared and able to comprehend and control its weight. James gives a word of Knowledge: (KJV)1:2-5 *My brethren, count it all joy when ye fall into divers temptations; Knowing this, that the trying of your faith worketh patience. But let patience have her perfect work, that ye may be perfect and entire, wanting nothing. If any of you lack wisdom, let him ask of God, that giveth to all men liberally, and upbraideth not; and it shall be given him.* With the emphasis on liberally, all may not get the same portion, but will receive the amount for which he has matured. Life brings the experiences and the testing for spiritual progress and the increase of wisdom. The Message: *Consider it a sheer gift, friends, when test and challenges come at you from all sides. You know that under pressure, your faith-life is forced into the open and shows its colors. So don't try to get out of anything pre-maturely. Let it do its work so you become mature and well developed, not deficient in any way. If you don't know what you're doing, pray to the Father. He loves to help. You'll get his help, and won't be condescended to when you ask for it.* Success may generate courage and promote confidence, but wisdom comes only from the experiences of adjustment to the results of one's failures.

Despair, Desertion, and the feeling of Depression; Jesus brings these three melancholy elements together as he so magnificently comes to the end of his first earthly mission. These three dreaded doors of progress and growth align themselves for the defense against inner weakness, introversions and insecurities. The by-products from these experiences and similar ones help bring a greater sense of hope, confidence and the ability to face life and enhance the ability to embrace love. We journey to and with the comfort of *Grace*, We encounter *Grief* in the climb, and through the process *Growth* takes place.

Chapter Five

The Passion of Daily Love

"I Thirst"
St John 19:28

The daily thirst to be comforted
The daily thirst for companionship
The daily thirst to be a channel

The Passion of Daily Love

"I Thirst"
John 19:28

Comfort, companionship, and being a channel are three elements that help give life fullness and meaning. These are some real human, tender, and practical sides of life and Love. This statement ***"I thirst"*** reminds us of these longings which are in every heart. It is the failure to fulfill these passions that can cause life to become boring and empty. It is also the presence of these elements that can help life to be full, productive and satisfying.

Thirst is a dry feeling in the throat that produces a desire to drink. I must say; if the horse is thirsty, when you lead him to the water, he *will* drink. This principle of drinking when thirsty may be used to point out what seems to be a lack of thirst in the collective passions of man as we may wonder why man is so unsatisfied, but the truth of the matter is man looks to the wrong sources to satisfy his desires. Man's thirst for knowledge is God given. It is the mind that God wants us to use to study and learn more ***about Him***. The emotional passions woven within the soul of man are also God given. It is these inner spiritual passions of the soul of which the Lord desires we use to worship and grow closer ***to Him***. When we consider the commands from God that we should love him with all our heart, with all our soul, and with all our might; it is the whole man including the physical body that He expects stewardship: development, maintenance, and presentation that we would walk ***with Him*** and freely live ***for Him***.

When we consider the cry from the cross we can relate to Jesus cry … I Thirst. *We see* ***first: The Daily Thirst to be Comforted.*** Every human being and many living creatures… long for a comforting touch. I am not aware of all the acts of animals, neither of the fish in the sea nor of the birds in the air. But, when we notice the character of God's creation, there is always activity comforting his handiworks. We see his welcoming comfort at the beginning of each day, when greeted by the freshness of the air, (Carbon Dioxide from the trees) and the warmth of his sunshine. He sends the rain at his will. The rain keeps the flying locusts from devouring the fruit of our labor so that when we plant seeds, the Lord protects the land for our harvest. We have such a comforting God and Father! Notice this one passage: Psalm 23:4 (KJV) "Yea, though I walk through the valley of the shadow of death, I will fear no evil: for thou art with me; thy rod and thy staff they comfort me."

The hand of God is continuously caring for his creatures. Those created and those made and created ("bara" original Hebrew scripture means to create out of nothing). One classic scripture gives us a reference to God's four sovereign acts of cosmic comforts. God maintains what he has made. *He **Created** (bara), he **Formed** (yatsar), he **Made** (asah), he **Established** (Kun).* Isaiah 45:18 (The Message), "God, Creator of the heavens – he is, remember, *God*. Maker of earth – he put it on its foundations, built it from scratch. He didn't go to all that trouble to leave it empty, nothing in it. He made it to be lived in." He made it to produce and to reproduce. Everything needed to produce life is in the earth.

There is a thirst to be satisfied deep in the soul of every man. It was put there by our creator to help drive us closer to him and to be willing to help comfort others. We are made in the image and likeness of God. We cannot deny that longing, we cannot deny that thirst. Men and woman, boys and girls reach out in many ways, seeking for comfort, Comfort from the loneliness of desertion, comfort from the pain of abuse, comfort from the lack of wisdom, the lack of strength and so much more.

The world we live in is hurting and need the comfort that only comes from a God of comfort. The search for comfort is looked for in many wrong places, people and passions. There is a divine command throughout the scriptures that we should comfort one another. Not only does the Bible instruct us to comfort, but gives us many words to use and the souls in which to apply them. The daily tragedy in far too many homes (really, there is no *home* without true comfort) is the fact that men and women have become too selfish, mean and cold hearted to be sensitive enough to use words of comfort. (KJV) Isaiah 40:1 "*Comfort ye, comfort ye my people, saith your God.* The Message Isaiah40: 2 "*Speak softly and tenderly to Jerusalem...*" The only way the thirst for comfort will be satisfied completely is in the Lord. It is the relationship with the eternal that satisfies the divine thirst of which every human soul longs. There is a daily thirst to be comforted when life brings to us the hurt of emotional pain from disappointments, delays, death, desertion, and destruction to name a few. There are more scriptures along this line. Comforting in a large way is done by the use of words; so the words that are use must have something that will bring a sense of relief, in a number of ways to a better understanding, an act or the knowledge of an act that brings comfort in some of at least three ways: the comfort of knowing, the comfort of hope, and the comfort of relief. When we hear the teachings from Apostle Paul in urging the Saints to comfort, it is to remind them to use certain words to do so. I Thessalonians 4:18 (KJV) "*Wherefore **comfort** one another with these words.*" It is the words of hope Paul refers concerning resurrection in contrast to the unbeliever; The Christians have hope of the resurrection at the face of death, the unbeliever, hopeless. Again in 5:11 *"Wherefore comfort yourselves together, and edify one another, even as also ye do."* There is a deep-seated need and passion in the heart of man to be comforted.

Jesus was in a position here thirsting for the comfort of mankind; the need to know that we can receive life in spite of the position of our birth, (born in sin wrapped in iniquity) in spite of the love of the world we have began to follow after, in spite of the love for the world, which is increasing, and in spite of our daily rebellious and renegade activity. This great love act takes away the power of sin from over our life by Christ becoming the payment and paying the penalty for sin of which Justice demands. Many may not realize their need for a savior; therefore, they will remain under the bondage of sin until the awakening. What we have under these conditions are the longings to be freed from sin, it is something going on in the inside of man, but he is not aware of the fact that it is the unrighteous position in which he stands. War is uncomfortable and as long as we are in bondage to the strong holds of satan, we stand in need of the comfort of freedom. Satan will continue to make us aware of our sin and use guilt without knowledge to keep us from surrendering fully to the Lord. Christ death on the cross has given us access to power greater than satan's over our life, but without that knowledge, we remain burden down with unnecessary pain. James The Message 4:7-10 "So let God work his will in you. Yell a loud *no* to the Devil and watch him scamper. Say a quiet *yes* to God and he'll be there in no time. Quit dabbling in sin. Purify your inner life. Quit playing the field. Hit bottom, and cry your eyes out. The fun and games are over. Get serious, really serious. Get down on your knees before the Master; it's the only way you'll get on your feet." We must keep in mind who we are, The Message, I John 4:4 "My dear children, you come from God and belong to God. You have already won a big victory over those false teachers, for the Spirit in you is far stronger than anything in the world." (KJV) "Ye are of God, little children, and have overcome them: because greater is he that is in you, than he that is in the world." From the recognition of such wretchedness to the realization of this marvelous salvation is the comfort of which man needs.

This thirst cry also covers the passion to be accompanied. It is **Secondly**: **The Daily Thirst for Companionship**.

Companionship is another element of life that is searched for in all the wrong places. Many have gone astray simply because of the wrong kind of company kept. When your days are empty of people to walk with, when there is no one with whom to genuinely share your interest and passions, the intimate side of life begins to starve for companionship and turns to anyone or anything to fill the void.

It is difficult to imagine here, but Christ spiritual thirst for companionship had to include the world's heart breaking weight of loneliness in walking this short but eternal road alone. It has been said that Jesus died of a broken heart, whether that's true or not; we certainly know that broken hearts come from the lack of companionship, having no one to walk with through the roads of life.

Companion is an intimate friend or associate, someone that has an interest in the same project or concern. Companionship can be lifelong or seasonal. I'm sure you have had someone commit to be with you through a certain challenge, project, and program or even in travel. We find examples in scripture that gives some insight of the value of companionship. Apostle Paul gives a few examples of the same. Acts 19:29 (KJV) …" *And the whole city was filled with confusion: and having caught Gaius and Aristarchus, men of Macedonia, Paul's* ***companions in travel****, they rushed with one accord into the theater."* (**Companion in labor**) (The Message) Philippians 2:25 … "*But for right now, I'm dispatching Epaphroditus, my good friend and* ***companionin my work.*** *You sent him to help me out; now I'm sending him to help you out."* (KJV) Revelation 1:9 *"I John, who also am your brother, and* ***companion in tribulation****, and in the kingdom and patience of Jesus Christ, was in the isle that is called Patmos, for the word of God, and for the testimony of Jesus Christ."* Now these are positive examples, but the scriptures also give warnings concerning keeping company with the wrong group. Here are some negatives: The Message Proverbs 13:20 *"Become* *wise by walking with the wise;* ***hang outwith fools*** *and watch your life fall to pieces" (KJV) "He that walketh with wise men shall be wise: but a* ***companion of fools*** *shall be destroyed."* Proverbs 28:7 "Whoso *keepeth the law is a wise son: but he that is a* ***companion of riotous*** *men shameth his father." 28:24 "Whoso robbeth his father or his mother and saith, It is no transgression; the same is the* ***companion of a destroyer****."* (The Message)Proverbs28: 7 "*Practice God's law-get a reputation for wisdom;* ***hang out with a loose crowd****-embarrass your family."* This is an urge and prayer that we do our best to hang out with those who chase after righteousness. The Prophet Amos asks the question: "*Can two walk together, except they be agreed?"* Apostle Paul says "*Be not deceived: evil communications corrupt good manners."*

This cry of thirst from Jesus Christ on the cross in a spiritual sense covers our daily passions mentally, emotionally and physically. The desire to be comforted when hurting and the desire to have companionship are both very natural and God given; however, the choices we make to fulfill these desires should be made through and with the guidance of divine wisdom.

Thirdly: We point to: **The Daily thirst to be a Channel.** Herein lies another one of God's spiritual and soulful implants, the passion to be a source of help be it counsel, inspiration, or lending a helping hand when needed. Since we were made in the image and likeness of God, we have that God like passion hidden deep in the moral fiber of our makeup; lined up like soldiers waiting for the command to engage in someone's life's struggles. You will find this passion to help in every innocent child, at the early "*let me help"* stage of life. It's found in the young man who gives up his seat for a lady on the bus or helps an old feeble person across a fast pass street, Its there in great relationships, with each trying to be there in support of the other's welfare. You will find that even as life approaches the wisdom ages, the passion to be a channel actually increases. Many men and women of age and wisdom wake up every morning seeking and praying for an opportunity to be a blessing to someone. They make themselves available for counsel, or to be a temporary companion through the episodes of life's daily struggles. Helpers are mentioned in the Bible. Here we have two classic cases when Moses was guided once by his father-in-law, (Exodus 18) and again by God (Numbers 11) to organize and choose men to help him in judging the people whom he led.

There is the gift of helps just as there are other gifts given to the Church, which is also called the Body of Christ for its maintenance and edification. I Corinthians 12:27-28, The Message: "You are Christ's body-that's who you are! You must never forget this. Only as you accept your part of that body does your "part" mean anything. You're familiar with some of the parts that God has formed in his Church, which is his "body": apostles, prophets, teachers, miracle workers, healers, ***helpers***, organizers, and those who pray in tongues." We can see that many of the gifts given in the Church were coveted more than others, which is the reason Apostle Paul had to write concerning this issue. It is important that we seek to please God in our efforts and from a pure heart. My point is that we all have a divine passion to be the channel, the source, or the conduit that brings either help, happiness, or healing to another. This passion as with many other righteous elements of life may lay dormant and inactive until whispered upon by Holy Spirit. While it is true we seek comfort and we seek companionship; when we consider the element of *being* a channel, we understand the other side, which is being that comfort for someone and that of being that companion for someone, this is aggressive ministry.

Daily Passions, for *Comfort* when hurting, for *Company* in life's journey, and to be a *Channel* of good as we travel are all divine inner cravings. The satisfaction of these three passions from this thirst cry are greatly acknowledged and pursued, wherefore companionship helps bring comfort, and there is a built in human element of compassion to help comfort those who are hurting, the desire to be a channel. It is when we give ourselves over to the work of Christ that we are fully satisfied and only when our work and motives are wrapped and woven in the love of God. The Efforts and the command to comfort comes here in (kJV) II Cor. 1:3,4 Blessed be God, even the Father of mercies, and the God of all comfort; Who comforted us in all our tribulation, that we may be able to comfort them which are in any trouble, by the comfort wherewith we ourselves are comforted of God. For as the sufferings of Christ abound in us, so our consolation also aboundeth by Christ.

Chapter Six

The Product Delivered is Love

"It is finished"
St John 19:30

The sacrifice of the innocent has been orchestrated
The satisfaction of justice has been obtained
The salvation for the sinner is now offered

The Product Delivered is Love

"It Is Finished"
John 19:30

Here we have another brief but powerful cry from the Lord Jesus Christ while on the cross of life and death. ***"It is finished"*** He has finished his first earthly mission in a grand and glorious style. Every detail, and every prophecy that was prophesied has been accomplished.

It has been a life without error lived with a passion to please his father in every assigned aspect. That which we have been privileged to read in holy writ brings joy, peace and salvation to the reader, and yet much or most of what he did; the world of books may not have been able to contain. It is finished now, and a retrospective view takes us into a life's history of divine beauty and as vast as the endless depths of combined oceans.

The Lord God Jehovah has finished the proof of his love toward man by the work of Jesus Christ on the cross at Calvary. It is finished! The actual assignment started on earth in the Garden of Eden, it was finished at Calvary's cross. The results of what he did for us as stated in: Galatians 3:13 (KJV) "Christ hath redeemed us from the curse of the law, being made a curse for us: for it is written, Cursed is every one that hangeth on a tree:" The emphasis of my point here is *for us*. God gave his Son *for us*, Christ gave his Life *for us*, we gave nothing but we must believe that these actions were made on our behalf in order to be received as a Christian by God. St John 1:12 (KJV) "But as many as received him, to them gave he power to become the sons of God, even to them that believe on his name:" The plan of salvation has been finished by this great love act of sacrificing the innocent (Jesus) for the guilty (us).

The road to finish is not an easy road, even in our everyday life. All along the life of Jesus were difficult challenges to face and overcome. The good news though concerning our earthly journey is the fact that we were born with all we need to do the same, *overcome.* Many things we can learn from our Lord's earthly life, but one thing for sure is God had a plan for his life way before he entered the planet. The plan of salvation and the presentation of a perfectly lived life as an example is why Christ came. Each, the plan of salvation and the life he lived have many lessons to be observed and absorbed. The plan of salvation is remarkable; we use words such as mysterious, in that it is a mystery how a heart of stone can be change into a heart of flesh, that is, a warm and caring heart. It is marvelous because no one else could have done such a spiritually beautiful thing. It is wonderful, in that it causes us to wonder how and why he would bring life to such a wretch like me. His plan included whosoever will; let him come, it also included a way for us to come boldly before the throne of grace and ask forgiveness for our daily sins. It has given us the power to live life at the highest point possible. And so: Here we see that it was his love for us, which made it possible for us to continue until our assigned work is complete. "*It is finished.*"

It is easy to make plans, all kinds of plans, but when the rubber meets the road or when the dreams of the heart meets the efforts of accomplishment, a separation takes place between those who dream and those who work at making dreams come true. This is a noble principle; for we may labor strong in life and still not reach our goals, but if we do, there is an assurance that our labor is not in vain. I must say here, It is the growth in wisdom of which we are seeking in every experience of life, whether it seems to be a failed or successful one, it is the wisdom gained from the experience that counts. I Corinthians 15:58 (KJV) "Therefore, my beloved brethren, be ye steadfast, unmovable, always abounding in the work of the Lord, forasmuch as ye know that your labor is not in vain in the Lord." The Message15:57, 58 "It was sin that made death so frightening and law-code guilt that gave sin its leverage, its destructive power. But now in a single victorious stroke of Life, all three—sin, guilt, death—are gone, the gift of our Master, Jesus Christ. Thank God! With all this going for us, my dear, dear friends, stand your ground. And don't hold back. Throw yourselves into the work of the Master, confident that nothing you do for him is a waste of time or effort." Many have difficulties in life because there are no clear plans to follow or a clear understanding of the purpose for their existence. It is the love of God that gives strength to continue. Let us keep in mind that "*The weak indulge in resolutions, but the strong act.* Life is but a day's work…do it well. The act is ours; the consequences God's." One more… Psalm 37:5,6 The Message "Open up before God, keep nothing back; he'll do whatever needs to be done: He'll validate your life in the clear light of day and stamp you with approval at high noon." (KJV) "Commit thy way unto the LORD; trust also in him; and he shall bring it to pass."

And so I think this discussion brings up at least three helpful principles to pursue. 1. ***Finding our Purpose from God*** *as* soon as possible, this is a parent responsibility in the early guidance of children. Bringing up our children in the nurture and admonition of the Lord is a strong mandate from the Lord. I must say here; that there are no guarantees that a child will embrace salvation, even when the best efforts have been made. The Message Proverbs 22:6 "Point your kids in the right direction – when they're old they won't be lost." If our children or we are to finish our assigned course, it is going to take guidance and strength found in the association with the Lord and the revealed instructions from scripture. Here is some of what Moses taught the nation of Israel concerning children on the plains of Moab: The Message: Deuteronomy 6: 3 …" Listen obediently, Israel. Do what you're told so that you'll have a good life, a life of abundance and bounty, just as GOD promised, in a land abounding in milk and honey. 5. Love God, your God, with your whole heart; love him with all that's in you, love him with all you've got! 6. Write these commandments that I've given you today on your hearts. Get them inside of you and then get them inside your children. Talk about them wherever you are, sitting at home or walking in the street; talk about them from the time you get up in the morning to when you fall into bed at night. Tie them on your hands and foreheads as a reminder; inscribe them on the doorposts of your homes and on your city gates." This kind of stuff is what it will take to walk through life and to finish with the passion, the peace and production God intended. 2. ***Fostering a Plan with God*** in which to attack life at the highest possible point, that of genuine agape Love, That of Wisdom, Education and Culture. Children are urged to get wisdom, and it would be so much easier to grow up around the pursuit of wisdom from a child in the family's environment. Timothy was fortunate to have grown up with a grandmother and a mother that loved the Lord. The World needs more praying and Godly parents today, a good question to ponder is: *What kind of parent am I or what kind of parent will I be?* Finishing well means getting a good start; at least it will increase a child's chances for success. 3. And being ***Faithful to Please God*** in all we do. We must be faithful until the end, until we cross the finish line, with honesty, perseverance and all that is within us. Love at its highest level constrains us to live like that. Colossians 3:16 Jesus quoted Moses from Deuteronomy 6:5 in (KJV) Matthew 22:37 when he said for us to "Love the Lord thy God with all thy heart, and with all thy soul, and with all thy mind."

Let's take a look at that which our Lord has cried out. It was a plan. It is now finished. It was a great benefit to the whole world. (KJV)John 3:16 … "For God so loved the world, that he gave his only begotten Son, that whosoever believeth in him should not perish, but have everlasting life."

From the viewpoint of a wretched man, Christ has performed a spiritual and physical miracle, both in this one magnificent act.

If we considered the miracle to be in three parts, the **First** part would be that: ***The sacrifice of the innocent has been orchestrated.*** God has so arranged things that even today the man in sin has another chance at life, the penalty for his sin has been paid, and he now has a right to continue working on the relationship, to get in the right standing between him and God.

I might need to briefly explain that this is the fulfillment of scripture in several ways. When Adam sinned in the Garden of Eden according to the scriptures, the death sentence came upon him and all born after Adam was born in sin; therefore we are all sinners at birth. We get scripture help and explanation here: Romans 5:12 (KJV) "...Wherefore, as by one man sin entered into the world, and death by sin; and so death passed upon all men, for that all have sinned:" 3:23 "for all have sinned, and come short of the glory of God;" Now if sin brought death, then death had to be paid. Adam sinned, but God took an innocent lamb, killed the lamb and accepted the death of the lamb as a payment for the sin that Adam had committed, until Adam was instructed to offer and repeat a sin sacrifice. Notice, if you will, it was an innocent lamb. If we were to pay for sin by dying, there would be no life. But God, who is rich in **mercy**, (holding back punishment that we deserve to get), arranged a way for a perfect lamb that would cover and abolish the sins of the world if we accept the provision by faith. In other words, we must believe God. We must keep in mind, when God sacrificed the lamb in the Garden of Eden; he took the skin of the lamb and covered the sin of Adam and Eve. That kind of sacrifice was practiced throughout the Old Testament times. Each time a sacrifice was made it pointed to Christ on the cross, the ultimate sacrifice which would end all others, for the sacrifices performed in the bible days were a temporary covering which needed to be accepted by God each time it was offered. It is the sovereign work of an eternal and compassionate God. Secondly we see that: ***The satisfaction of justice has been obtained.***

Justice is the part of God's personality that holds the strength of his promises to be a God that does not waver. It is the cosmic watchman who foresees and oversees every gift of grace and every act of mercy. Justice is the ultimate fair exchange to righteous motives and pure heart efforts, as well as the paymaster for the lawbreaker and the apostasy. The Lord extends **mercy,** and the Lord extends **grace**, but never at the expense of **justice**. He will always be fair and righteous according to his own nature. If we think about it, that is exactly what he has done on the cross with Jesus, in connection with the sin and sins of the world for those who believe and receive him as their personal Savior. We sinned, like Adam, so Jehovah God extended mercy by not killing us, He also extended grace by allowing us a way to life, but then justice was satisfied because an innocent lamb (Christ Jesus) was slain to pay the price of our sin. Again we go to Romans 6:23, 24 (KJV) "For the wages of sin is death, but the gift of God is eternal life through Jesus Christ our Lord." We must also be reminded of the fact that we are saved, not by our works or anything else other than the grace of God and our decision to believe and accept Christ as our personal savior. **Thirdly** we conclude in a short version that: ***The salvation for the sinner is now offered.*** This is an exciting statement when we understand the penalty that was paid for us. There is one thing for sure and understandably so, the thief that Christ saved while hanging on the cross certainly got it. The sad reality though, just like the other sinner, hanging as close to Christ as the other, many men today will be lost while Christ is just a call away. *I plead with you, the reader; don't be like the thief who died in his sin while Christ the Savior was just a call away!* The Lord has set the table of life for life, to all that will be saved. It is not the Lord's will that any would be lost, but here again, many will refuse to believe. Salvation is now offered, the opportunity for man to be reconciled (to be in good fellowship) with God based on our position at birth. The Message, Romans 5: 8-10 … "He presented himself for this sacrificial death when we were far too weak and rebellious to do anything to get ourselves ready. And even if we hadn't been weak, we wouldn't have known what to do anyway. We can understand someone dying for a person worth dying for, and we can understand how someone good and noble could inspire us to selfless sacrifice. But god put his love on the line for us by offering his Son in sacrificial death while we were of no use whatever to him." The Psalmist says: (KJV)"Behold, I was shapen in iniquity; and in sin did my mother conceive me." This great love operation here on the tree on Golgotha's hill has taken away the power of sin from over our life by Christ Jesus becoming the payment for our sins and paying the price of the penalty (Death) for our sins of which Justice demands. The difference is this: The Message Romans 6:23 "Work hard for sin your whole life and your pension is death. But God's gift is real life, eternal life, delivered by Jesus, our Master." This part of Christ earthly mission has been in his own words, "*It is finished*" All of these discussions are connected in the one act, and though we have several lessons from his historical statements, and the events that took place at Calvary were prophesied in old scripture, this is the *one love episode* that opens the freedom door to eternal life.

Chapter Seven

The Place to Deposit Love

"Father, into your hands I commend my spirit"
Luke 23: 46

The entrance of an eternal cause
The establishment of an enduring comfort
The epitome of an extreme challenge

The Place to Deposit Love

"Father, into your hands I commend my spirit
Luke 23: 46

This is the end of the first earthly and difficult mission but the beginning of an eternal cause. It had to be the worst earthly experience for our savior while accomplishing the best thing that could have ever happened to mankind.

Our body goes back to the ground while our spirit goes back to God from whence it came. It is also crucial for us to consider the legacy we leave behind. Many of us have considered the lessons of the dash between the date of birth and the date of departure carved on the headstones in cemeteries.

Those of us who are serious about life want to leave something behind that will benefit others in a eternal and spiritual way. It is kingdom work, the words of inspiration, spoken or written. We want to leave some memories that last, planted deep in the reservoir of a hungry soul, to be brought up and used over and over whenever life brings the temptation to quit, to get revenge or to act on any other imposter that rises against the progresses of life.

The emphasis here is on what has been accomplished during our earthly sojourn. The questions are, did we ever show up for class, and if we did how was our focus in regards to the teachings and the teacher? If we showed up and got something from class, did we put it to work for us? If we accomplished anything worthwhile, what was our attitude toward others in regard to status?

There is the **personal behavior** and attitude toward life and then there is the **relational behavior.** It is a fact that the Lord made man to work, he is built to labor at the sweat of his face. Man's success for the most part depends on his **personal**

behavior towards life and work. The accomplishments of our life depend on the preparations through education, our willingness to study and learn from life lessons.

Most everyone wants to succeed financially in life, but not everyone has either the discipline or the opportunity to pursue in-depth training and formal education. We can become an educated person with the ability to do well for ourselves and actually be in a position to be a blessing to others; but the attitude and the relational behavior as to how we relate to others can cause people to shun our presence based on how we make them feel. We must be careful in how we treat others regardless of their status in life. Our relational skills and our heart may not be one of a charitable platform. True prosperity and true success is never selfish and cold hearted. We are reminded throughout the scriptures how we should care for others and be willing to share a word of comfort whenever opportunity shows up. Love is not a natural gift; the carnal man cannot love the way God has commanded. It is a learning process and a daily practice even after we have been born again as a Christian; however, the things that count with God most, in connection to our living, is our genuine efforts in relating to others, how purely we put love into action, and the attitude in which we did.

Like love wealth is not a natural gift; it results from labor, knowledge, and organization. Wealth principles are wonderful to practice, and should be practiced with passion, but whatever your wealthy status may be; it's nothing in the scheme of real life without the consistent application of agape Love.

We must not find ourselves operating under the "me, myself, and mine" mode of living. You know, it's hard for me to do something for someone else unless I am seen by many and get my proper praise for doing so. After all I have sacrificed my time and used my education and my own money to help. People need to know what a wonderful person I am. The next thing is I must be in control or else I don't think it is something I want to fully support. I must be the head for I just cannot and will not allow someone to show me, teach me, or even suggest something to me that I won't get the most credit. I believe in helping people. I believe in going to church and worshiping God as long as I am seen. I will sit and be taught as long as it appears that I am somebody special in the crowd. I can criticize anybody I feel like. But I dare someone find a fault with me. I can explain it and when I'm finish, you will clearly see that it was not my fault and that in fact most of the time my shortcomings are due to the actions of someone else. My feelings are very thin; so don't try to point out my errors. Of course, when I want to say something about someone or to someone else, their feeling does not matter. Real life strongly suggests we not live like that.

We have here before us a life that brought the greatest change in the history of mankind, from the very beginning of our existence. The acme of earthly living has been demonstrated in a marvelous and magnificent manner.

The purpose for which he came was accomplished, and though his statement was to bring life and to bring it more abundantly, (St John 10:10 (KJV) *"…I am come that they might have life, and that they might have **it** more abundantly.")* the benefits from his life immeasurable, the beauty of his life unparalleled, and that brings us so much more. The burdens of life, which he lifted, were before unthinkable.

The **first** point of his legacy is that he created: ***The entrance of an eternal cause.*** All that Jesus has done is now committed into the hands of the LORD from which he came. What he has accomplished and the legacy of his life are now His-story. He has brought to us a cause that will be chronicled in the archives of eternity.

We must know that without the life and the cross of Christ man would still be in his sin and doomed to die no matter what.

It is the cause of Christ for which he died. The cause of Christ however is the salvation of the world or whosoever will. (KJV) St. John 3:16 *"For God so loved the world that he gave his only begotten Son, that whosoever believeth in him should not perish, but have everlasting life."* The Message St John 3: 16 *"this is how much God loved the world: He gave his Son, his one and only Son. And this is why: so that no one need be destroyed; by believing in him, anyone can have a whole and lasting life."*

This is an eternal entrance into the door of life which could not have happen without this act of Love that goes beyond the comprehension of the mortal mind, the ability or the passion of our finite existence and human understanding. It transcends our discernment and deserving. It is the grace and mercy of God's personality, managed by his omnipotent sovereignty and Justice. There is **secondly** the fact that he has given us: ***The establishment of an enduring comfort.*** If we were to say that Christ came to comfort man, we would be correct, for everything done is certainly a great comfort to mankind if he would only believe it and receive it. Previously we discussed the presence of a daily thirst in every soul, and a thirst to be comforted was included. There is now an enduring comfort for those who have learned to trust in God. The great news about this enduring comfort is that it is there for the asking, continuously, whenever we want to call, it has been established throughout eternity.

There is a difference in the view of these two discussions of comfort: The former in chapter five points to the fact that we need and desire comfort when we are hurting as a human being. That includes the spirit man as well as the physical body, comfort means there is someone who cares enough for us when we hurt to either be there and sympathies with us, who may get help, or someone who have the skills to help. Here, we see that *that comfort* has been established and done so for eternity.

Christ has left this enduring comfort behind and is now entrusting it into the hands of God. There is great comfort in knowing that we no longer have to face death because of what Adam did. There is comfort in knowing the Love of God has brought salvation to us and the abundant life along with it. There is comfort in knowing we can walk with the Lord daily by way of the Holy Spirit. We can call on the Lord when we have a special need for anything, that's a great comfort. There is a comfort in knowing that the one who loves us is able to comfort our hurts and deliver our needs. He is omnipotent, which means he is able, he is omnipresent, which means he is there no matter where we are and he is omniscient which means he knows all about our problem.

The earthly legacy of Christ brings to mankind an opportunity to live life in the manner that can be pleasing to God. His work or legacy has left an opportunity for man to be productive, pleasing, and peaceful while living in a self-centered and messed up world. There are a few words of which will give comfort in knowing. It is a joy and comfort in knowing that "The earth is the Lord's and the fullness thereof;" "It is a comfort in knowing that, "The Lord is my shepherd; I shall not want." It is a Joy and comfort in knowing that "greater is he that is within me than he that is within the world.

There are many scriptures that bring comfort by knowing the truth of them, but I also want to stress the importance of having the right relationship with the Lord. All of what we have discussed here means little to the one who have not made the decision to walk aggressively with the Lord. This comfort is available; but it is not automatic; in other words God has done his part by providing us a way to live life and to live it more abundantly, (that is the reason Christ came) but we have to seek the Lord and receive him as our own personal Lord and daily walk with him.

We look now at the point of discussion, which brings up the *effort* in which Jesus carried out his mission. We see that not only did he establish the entrance of an eternal cause, and not only was there the establishment of an enduring comfort, but thirdly we note: ***The Epitome of an Extreme Challenge*** The things which were set before the Lord Jesus to accomplish were extremely difficult, but not only were they extremely difficult to accomplish, the way he finished and the way he carried out his work was magnificently done. Here, again from The Message Hebrews 12:2 "Keep your eyes on *Jesus,* who both began and finished this race we're in. Study how he did it. Because he never lost sight of where he was headed-that exhilarating finish in and with God-he could put up with anything along the way: Cross, shame, whatever. And now he's *there*, in the place of honor, right alongside God." ("When you find yourselves flagging in your faith, go over that story again, item by item, that long litany of hostility he plowed through. *That* will shoot adrenaline into your souls!" It was an example on how to live life under the most extreme pressures and sometimes conditions.

The work that was set before him was also not easy because he had to train and teach men who were not well-learned men. They were not college professors or even great scholars of any sort; they were good men who were in the fishing business. The evidence of Jesus persuasive teaching shows up in the Disciples' power and boldness in their proclamations of the Gospel and the healings made among the people. Acts 4:13 (KJV) "Now when they saw the boldness of Peter and John, and perceived that they were unlearned and ignorant men, they marveled; and they took knowledge of them, that they had been with Jesus." The Message "They couldn't take their eyes off them-Peter and John standing there so confident, so sure of themselves! Their fascination deepened when they realized these two were laymen with no training in Scripture or formal education. They recognized them as companions of Jesus," Here we see the great impact of how well taught and how deeply empowered were those who Jesus touched, and those who received his Spirit.

Another thing is that the lessons that needed to be taught these men were almost unheard of and understood, not only by these men, but even the scholars of that day had not heard or seen a man teach the things that Jesus taught. They also never witnessed a man who taught *the way* Jesus taught, his style, his wording, and his level of confidence in which he brought out his points. It was then a masterful example of how a man will live when he has the fullness of God's spirit within him, guiding his mind and sustaining his will to make the right decisions and to do the right things. In this passage concerning Jesus we read, St John 7:46 The Message "The police answered, "Have you heard the way he talks? We've never heard anyone speak like this man." When we read and understand the upgraded lifestyle presented by Jesus Christ; I don't know about you, but I get inspired to be better in every walk of life, After all, his life is an example for us to follow and gives some assurance that overcoming obstacles and finishing our divine assignment is certainly possible.

The other half of that statement; *The Epitome of an Extreme Challenge* is the fact that *what* Jesus was teaching was not only not heard of, but it was not very popular by main stream society and therefore was resisted and it was resisted aggressively. The message that Christ brought to the world found strong resistance from three groups: The society. Including those in business who may stood to lose economically, satan, who from the beginning and even now uses men and demons to try to alter Christ's plans or to hinder the works of the Lord. There were also the Politicians, the high religious leaders such as the Pharisees and Sadducees and the politicians of that day. These men fought Jesus concerning customs, Mosaic laws, and the lack of understanding concerning the coming Messiah, of which they refused to believe that Jesus was He, among other things. Jesus Christ was and is also in today's society a great disturbance to these personalities who became uncomfortable and who are uncomfortable with the presence and the presentations of this Jesus. I need you to keep in mind that because we are walking in the footsteps Jesus, the world will likewise become uncomfortable with you and me. I have a slight smile on my face when I say that, because I know that many Christians struggle with standing out with boldness in the light of Christian principles.

Now if I can paint this picture clearly for you, it may give you a small idea of the monumental task set before our Lord and again the splendid manner in which he accomplished it.

I think I need to tell you, that Holy Spirit, when we receive him, will do the same for us; it may not get us to live as perfectly as did Jesus, But he will cause us to appear as if we are following in the footsteps of our Lord Jesus; and that is exactly what the Lord want us to do and look like. We can certainly remain under the umbrella of righteousness by using the tool of scriptures with a pure heart. When we miss the mark; The Lord has given us the grace of forgiveness. I John 1:9... (KJV) "If we confess our sins, he is faithful and just to forgive us our sins, and to cleanse us from all unrighteousness." Also Proverbs 28:13 (KJV) "He that covereth *(Continues to keep)* his sins shall not prosper: but whoso confesseth *(Continues to ask forgiveness to God)* and forsaketh *(Continues to run from)* them shall have mercy." This grace will help us stay in good fellowship with our Father God. Herein is the perfection of which the Lord commands of us: From the great teachings called the Sermon on the Mount; Jesus ends with this command, Matthew5:48 ... "Be ye therefore perfect, even as your Father which is in heaven is perfect." Also in The Message "In a word, what I'm saying is, *Grow up*. You're kingdom subjects. Now live like it. Live out your God-created identity. Live generously and graciously toward others, the way God lives toward you." If we are to finish with a legacy of righteousness, we are to continue asking The Lord through prayer for forgiveness anytime we do wrong. Apostle Paul confesses in: Acts 24:16 (KJV) "And herein do I exercise myself to have always a conscience void of offense toward God, and *toward* men." Also The Message: "Believe me; I do my level best to keep a clear conscience before God and my neighbors in everything I do."

The Gospel writers gave several references when the LORD made known his pleasure concerning the performance of Jesus while on his earthly mission. It was at Jesus' baptism by John the Baptist when the audible voice of God announced and acknowledged Jesus as his beloved Son in whom he was well pleased; again at the mountain of transfiguration when the LORD announced, "This is my beloved Son, in whom I am well pleased; hear ye him."

And so Jesus Christ submits his life into the hands of Jehovah God, The Almighty God, The Eternal God, The Infinite, The Living, The Everlasting, Most High Only Potentate; the God of Goodness, the God of Holiness and Impartiality, the God of Mercy, Grace and Truth. The God of Omnipotence, Omnipresence and Omniscience; the Only Wise God, the God of Love. … Well … This Great God, the Father of our Lord and Savior, Jesus Christ. These are the best hands to which we too can submit our life. He can do more with it than we. I urge you, the reader to strongly consider the Lord's plan for your life today. It is the only way to have true earthly and *eternal good* success.

Chapter Eight

The Conclusion of the Whole Matter

A Splendid sojourn filled with

A Passion of unusual Persuasion
A Presentation for universal Peace
A Purity of uncompromising Principles

In the last discussion we talked about the Master's work on earth, yet his divine assignment as it relates to salvation. Here; as best I can without being too redundant I want to point out the Master's life on earth as it culminated on the cross in light of the universe, if you will. And, I want to identify the direction of his life in at least three views. It is the eternal legacy of his life, and the universal color of his works, both of which history embrace the *significance and power* his life brought to mankind.

Before I begin discussion of the outlined point of this chapter; let's take note of the direction of his life. Here are at least three principles of success, which over-shadowed the life of Jesus. These success principles presented are what I call *attitude principles.* They are the attitude of *Sacrifice*, (Giving oneself for others) the attitude of *Submission*, (Obedience to the highest laws) and the attitude of the *Servant.* (Joyfully doing for others) One of their common threads is that the practice of each must come from a decision to do so, and must be practiced from the heart.

What a *wonder-full* journey (with the emphasis on both) Christ Jesus had on the planet during this incarnation. A Splendid sojourn, and filled with the great love of God. (The Agape Love) It is that of saving those who are lost, past, present and the future. What a wonder his life must have been to those who walked with him and those who encountered his presence during his sojourn; and the other thing is the life packed full of activity according to the scriptures and the confession of the writers, "maybe the world could not have contained his total activities."

We see clearly that this great act presented to us is first: ***Sacrificial;*** *Remember* without Sacrificing we neither grow in character nor gain in content. Sacrificing is a basic and fundamental part of life's progress, it is the time giver in developing the God given skills within us, and it is part of the glue that holds together each brick of a productive life. Sacrificing is necessary whether we are developing ourselves to become physically fit, or going out of our way to help a needy soul. It is necessary for increasing expert knowledge, and called for in the sacrifice of praise to God in the maintenance and consistency of our spiritual growth. A note of scripture here: Paul in writing to the Church at Rome, gives a doxology of praise to God's wisdom, and reasons why sacrificing for the Christian should be a fundamental and daily activity. He reminds us in Romans 33-36, The Message: "Have you ever come on anything quite like this extravagant generosity of God, this deep, deep wisdom? It's way over our heads. We'll never figure it out. Is there anyone around who can explain God? Anyone smart enough to tell him what to do? Anyone who has done him such a huge favor that God has to ask his advice? Everything comes from him; everything happens through him; everything ends up in him. Always glory! Always praise! Yes. Yes. Yes." Romans 12:1-2 (KJV) "I beseech you ***therefore***, brethren, by the mercies of God, that ye present your bodies a ***living sacrifice***, holy, acceptable unto God, which is your reasonable service. And be not conformed to this world: but be ye transformed by the renewing of your mind that ye may prove what is that good, and acceptable, perfect, will of God." Also The Message: "So here's what I want you to do, God helping you: Take your everyday, ordinary life--- your sleeping, eating going-to-work, and walking around life- and place it before God as an offering, Embracing what God does for you is the best thing you can do for him. Don't become so well adjusted to your culture that you fit into it without even thinking. Instead, fix your attention on God. You'll be changed from the inside out. Readily recognize what he wants from you, and quickly respond to it. Unlike the culture around you, always dragging you down to its level of immaturity, God brings the best out of you, develops well-formed maturity in you.

I'm speaking to you out of deep gratitude for all that God has given me, and especially as I have responsibilities in relation to you. Living then, as every one of you does, in pure grace, it's important that you not misinterpret yourselves as people who are bringing this goodness to God. No, God brings it all to you. The only accurate way to understand ourselves is by what God is and by what he does for us, not by what we are and by what we do for him."

Life is filled with the opportunities to sacrifice. Sacrificing is one of the inner elements that bring an outer glow. Secondly, there is the principle of ***Submission***. This is not a very popular principle to practice because it means we must give up our will to that of another person or cause.

When and if we consider the benefits that are hidden from the immediate appearance in obeying, it will become easier to lay aside our own will to that of God's divine purpose for our life. Submission means obedient to the *commands* of God, obedient to the *rules* in the home, and obedient to the *laws* of the land, but the benefits that follow will last throughout life.

You know that submission is not always a good thing. Let me also point out the fact that although submission seems to be a dreaded principle, men have voluntarily become subservient to many deadly strongholds.

Whenever the principle of submission *is* practiced, it is in pursuit to exercise either the **principles of faith,** the **pressures of fear** or the **passions for fun.** People have been persuaded to submit and participate in many deadly and dangerous activities, both physically and spiritually. It is the choices we decide to make, which bring the consequences we receive. The Lord has set before us a choice of life and death. The bible says it like this St. Jn. 3:19 (KJV) "And this is the condemnation, that light is come into the world, and men loved darkness rather than light, because their deeds were evil."

Christ demonstrates by his life the acme of many lessons, and submission is certainly at the top of the list. We see here the mind of his father, the will and the plans of his father all performed at the highest point possible. One of the great joys of any master teacher is to see his student perform precisely as he was taught. And just as Jesus' performance pleased his father, we as his children should also strive to please him. And so; our life's aim and encouragement should be: Ephesians 5:15-21 (KJV) … "See then that ye walk circumspectly, not as fools, but as wise, Redeeming the time, because the days are evil. Wherefore be ye not unwise, but understanding what the will of the Lord *is*. And be not drunk with wine, wherein is excess; but be filled with the Spirit; Speaking to yourselves in psalms and hymns and spiritual songs, singing and making melody in your heart to the Lord; Giving thanks always for all things unto God and the Father in the name of our Lord Jesus Christ; ***Submitting*** ourselves one to another in the fear of God." The Message11-21 … "Don't waste your time on useless work, mere busywork, the barren pursuits of darkness. Expose these things for the sham they are. It's a scandal when people waste their lives on things they must do in the darkness where no one will see. Rip the cover off those frauds and see how attractive they look in the light of Christ. Wake up from your sleep, Climb out of your coffins; Christ will show you the light! So watch your step. Use your head. Make the most of every chance you get. These are desperate times! Don't drink too much wine. That cheapens your life. Drink the Spirit of God, huge draughts of him. Sing hymns instead of drinking songs! Sing songs from your heart to Christ. Sing praises over everything, and any excuse for a song to God the Father in the name of our Master, Jesus Christ.

Thirdly we are presented with the principle of ***Serving.*** One of the last and direct lessons Jesus gave his disciples near the end of his first earthly mission was that of Serving. The great lesson the Master demonstrated by washing his disciple's feet; had strong emphasis on the attitude of a servant. (St. John 13:5 (KJV) "After that he poureth water into a basin, and began to wash the disciples' feet, and to wipe them with the towel wherewith he was girded.")When serving from the point of love, humility is not far away; for true service takes away the selfish motives and fills the attitude of our activity with the comfort, support, and the inspiration of another.

We look now at the eternal legacy of this extraordinary life, Gift, Savior and Teacher. Christ waste no time in selecting students that would become the apostles of the doctrines of which he taught. This was an unusual selection in the light of whom he chose. We must note that in the days of Christ Jesus physical earthly presence, the rabbis or Priests of those days were men well respected and their position highly desired. It was the priest; however, who would choose the students who wish to be taught under them. Under most customs, the Priest would frequent a school of divinity and make a choice of the best students, who would then be assigned studies and memory work, from this group they would choose the best of the best for a worthy student understudy. This selection proved to be a ***Passion of an unusual Persuasion,*** for these men not only changed the direction of their own life's; but the one Divine call from Christ Jesus persuaded and influenced the hand full of disciples to grab hold of the eternal message and virtually change the course of the world.

The true message has never died out or dried out, it has never shaded or shifted, nor has it been proven ineffective when rightly applied. This same message of Life and Hope has persuaded many lost soul throughout the ages. It has healed many sick, mended many broken hearts and lifted many downtrodden spirits. It has truly been a Passion of unusual Persuasion from the heart of God through Christ Jesus.

When Jesus first began his ministry, he performed many miracles, healed the sick of different physical problems and many other works and gave great words of wisdom that was not heard before but could not be disputed. These activities gave Jesus a reputation and an obvious priestly position from the works of which he did. It was by his works that drew Nicodemus to him at night to inquire of him concerning religion, salvation and the steps it takes to become a Christian. Nicodemus was not alone, there were many who could not deny the wonderful and practical works of Jesus; but there hung a mystery cloud of faith as to how he did what was done and should they believe him to be real or not.

Not only did the Life of Christ bring to the universe *A Passion of Unusual Persuasion*, but it also proved to be ***A Presentation for universal Peace.*** Just to make sure, this peace was brought to the world in the person of Jesus, whom scripture prophesy called The Prince of Peace. Jesus declares; St. John 14:7 (KJV) "Peace I leave with you, my peace I give unto you: not as the world giveth, give I unto you. Let not your heart be troubled, neither let it be afraid." Also Philippians 4:7 "And the peace of God, which passeth all understanding, shall keep your hearts and minds through Christ Jesus."

The world cannot experience this kind of peace because it only comes through Christ Jesus whom they rejected at his entrance and aggressively reject him even today.

The life of Jesus brought to us the real root and core of what it means to have real peace, peace in every aspect of life. He brought to us Peace for the inner man ... personal peace, peace for our past and peace for our present feeble efforts of daily struggles at becoming perfect. Real peace has a root from which it grows. We are not born with the ability to understand peace nor are we able to experience the joy peace brings without the relationship with Christ who is the true source of peace; And when we receive Christ as our personal Lord and savior, we receive the source or the root of peace. Isaiah calls him a root out of a dry ground. 53:2 "For he shall grow up before him as a tender plant, and as a root out of a dry ground..." He is the core of the Christian's life, buried deep in the center of the heart and mind of the every true believer, giving substance and illumination to the countenance. He is waiting to be stirred up and nurtured from the increase of knowledge of the word, from the practice of prayer and from the exercise of meditation.

As simple as it may seem, some of the most important elements of life must be learned. Peace is like love; it has to be pursued, embraced and practiced. Hebrews 12:14 (KJV) "**Follow peace** with all *men*, and holiness, without which no man shall see the Lord:" Psalm 34:14 "Depart from evil, and do good; **seek peace and pursue it."** Romans 14:19 "Let us therefore **follow after** the things which make for **peace**, and things wherewith one may edify another." It is the practice that causes growth to occur in all of life's crucial character builders. One of the Beatitudes' of which Christ taught on the mountain declares that, Happy is the Peacemakers: for they shall be called the children of God.

I really must stop a moment and emphasize the all of this peace talk is a presentation from God by Christ Jesus. It is not automatically given to us; we must reach out and embrace it. It is our choice and choosing to accept or reject. Peace is available; Love is also, and when we accept them, the rich and many benefits come too.

There is also a presentation for universal peace wrapped up in Christ; for if mankind understood the power of the pursuit of peace, the joy, the power of agape love, and each soul labored to achieve these divine gifts, then the world could experience the peace of God on a national and worldwide scale. Okay, I know … sounds like fantasy. This will not happen here and now, because of the rejection of Christ Jesus and what he brought to the world. Jesus taught that the poor would always be with us; and that there would be an increase number of tragedies based on the ramification of sin. This world we live in is not pro-Christ, but rebels against every cause of Christ and against everyone that strives to represent him. Yes; there is a wonderful presentation of peace, full of life's principles that could make this a wonderful place to live; but this world and planet in which we exists is satan's territory and there is no way he will allow peace to go unchallenged. He will try to get as many as he can deceive to follow him to eternal damnation.

The Bible urges and exhorts men to accept Christ, love him and passionately live for him. Paul in Colossians 3:2 "Set your affections on things above, not on things on the earth." 3:15 "… And let (give permission) the peace of God rule in your hearts, to the which also ye are called in one body; and be ye thankful." The Message 3:15, 16 "Let the peace of Christ keep you in tune with each other, in step with each other; None of the going off and doing your own thing. And cultivate thankfulness. Let the Word of Christ-the message-have the run of the house. Give it plenty of room in your lives. Instruct and direct one another using good commonsense. And sing; sing your hearts out to God! Let every detail in your lives-words, actions whatever-be done in the name of the Master, Jesus, thanking God the Father every step of the way." I John 2:15 "Don't love the world's ways. Don't love the world's goods. Love of the world squeezes out love for the Father. Practically everything that goes on in the world-wanting your own way, wanting everything for yourself, wanting to appear important-has nothing to do with the Father. It just isolates you from him. The world and all it's wanting, wanting, wanting is on the way out- but whoever does what God wants is set for eternity." The few that choose Christ are the few that will receive an inheritance with Christ; as you may remember in the previous chapter, Christ promised the Thief a place in Paradise. We too are promised life eternally with The LORD.

Lest I bore you, let us consider our final discussion of this magnificent life, for not only was his life a splendid sojourn filled with a Passion of unusual Persuasion and A Presentation for universal Peace, but it at least was also filled with **A Purity**

of uncompromising Principles. He was not conniving; he was not trying to get over, neither was he deceitful; there were no ulterior motives. He was honest and upfront about the way he lived and taught. The Lord cannot be tempted to make unfair judgments or commit an unjust act. His actions were bold, his speech confident, for he had no guilt or shame to hide.

We have in Christ Jesus the greatest example of a pure heart; which produces pure motives, and brings to us the purest love possible, even agape love. The good thing about Christ's purity is that it cannot be persuaded to turn even at a shadow. Love is not real unless it is pure and without strings attached. Love cannot lead or persuade one against Godly principles or any life giving principles. Love is pure and filled with wholesome intents only. Pure gold and perfect diamonds are uncompromising when it comes to true value; and Our Christian walk should be pointing in that direction, no wavering *in our hearts* with the indecision of whether I'm going to do right.

When we sin, and come to God, he knows what happen and why we sinned, but he wants us to acknowledge, confess and repent. When we sin, in our hearts we become very sorrowful; and when we confess and repent, the Lord wipes away the stain of sin from our record based on the blood of Jesus Christ who died for our sins.

Here we have the perfect love filled with grace, mercy and righteous judgment, the wholesome intent toward us for our benefit.